MEDICAL PRACTICE MANAGEMENT

Body of Knowledge Review

VOLUME 5

Human Resource Management

Michael A. O'Connell, MHA, FACMPE, CHE

Managing Editor

Lawrence F. Wolper, MBA, FACMPE

Medical Group
Management
Association

Medical Group Management Association
104 Inverness Terrace East
Englewood, CO 80112-5306
877.275.6462
Website: www.mgma.com

Production Credits

Executive Editor: Andrea M. Rossiter, FACMPE

Managing Editor: Lawrence F. Wolper, MBA, FACMPE

Editorial Director: Marilee E. Aust

Production Editor: Marti A. Cox, MLIS

Substantive and Copy Editor: Sandra Rush, Rush Services

Proofreaders: Scott Vickers, InstEdit and Karen Krizman

Fact Checking: Mary S. Mourar, MLS

Page Design, Composition and Production: Boulder Bookworks

Cover Design: Ian Serff, Serff Creative Group, Inc.

PUBLISHER'S CATALOGING IN PUBLICATION DATA

O'Connell, Michael A.
    Human resource management / by Michael A. O'Connell ; managing editor Lawrence F. Wolper. – Englewood, CO : MGMA, 2006.
    132 p. ; cm. – (Medical Practice Management Body of Knowledge Review Series ; v. 5)
Includes index.
ISBN 1-56829-236-8
    1. Human resources. 2. Medical offices – Personnel management. [LC] 3. Personnel management – methods [MeSH]. I. Wolper, Lawrence F. II. Medical Group Management Association. III. American College of Medical Practice Executives. IV. Series. V. Series: Body of Knowledge Review Series.

R728.O26 2006
610.68—dc22   2005938860

Item 6357

ISBN: 1-56829-236-8   Library of Congress Control Number: 2005938860

Acknowledgments

To my wife, Marianne, for her constant love and for her support of my professional career, and to my children, Matthew, Molly, Andrew, and Nora, for keeping me focused on family.

To my parents, Barney and BJ, for their solid values and constant encouragement to continuously learn.

To my first physician mentor, John J. Collins Jr., MD, who demonstrated, through example, the pursuit of quality patient care in a caring, compassionate, and cost-effective way.

To Hansel Foley, MD, a family practice physician who gave 150 percent to his patients and their health concerns. He kept me focused on the importance of how to build a medical practice through respect, hard work, and excellent service.

And to A. Gus Kious, MD, an enthusiastic and passionate physician and administrator committed to providing superior medical care to an underserved community.

Contents

Series Overview

THE MEDICAL GROUP MANAGEMENT ASSOCIATION (MGMA) serves medical practices of all sizes, as well as management services organizations, integrated delivery systems, and ambulatory surgery centers to assist members with information, education, networking, and advocacy. Through the American College of Medical Practice Executives® (ACMPE®), MGMA's standard-setting and certification body, the organization provides board certification and Fellowship in medical practice management and supports those seeking to advance their careers.

■ **Core Learning Series: A professional development pathway for competency and excellence in medical practice management**

Medical practice management is one of the fastest-growing and most rewarding careers in health care administration. It is also one of the most demanding, requiring a breadth of skills and knowledge unique to the group practice environment. For these reasons, MGMA and ACMPE have created a comprehensive series of learning resources, customized to meet the specific professional development needs of medical practice managers: the Medical Practice Management Core Learning Series.

The Medical Practice Management Core Learning Series is a structured approach that enables practice administrators and staff to build the core knowledge and skills required for career success. Series resources include seminars, Web-based education programs, books, and online assess-ment tools. These resources provide a strong, expansive foundation for managing myriad job responsibilities and daily challenges.

■ Core Learning Series: Resources for understanding medical practice operations

To gain a firm footing in medical practice management, executives need a broad understanding of the knowledge and skills required to do the job. The Medical Practice Management Core Learning Series offers "Level 1" resources, which provide an introduction to the essentials of medical practice management. As part of the learning process, professionals can use these resources to assess their current level of knowledge across all competency areas, identify gaps in their education or experience, and select areas in which to focus further study. The *Medical Practice Management Body of Knowledge Review Series* is considered to be a Core Learning Series – Level 1 resource.

Level 1 resources meet the professional development needs of individuals who are new to or considering a career in the field of medical practice management, assuming practice management responsibilities, or considering ACMPE board certification in med-ical practice management.

Also offered are Core Learning Series – Level 2 resources, which provide exposure to more advanced concepts in specific compe-tency areas and their application to day-to-day operation of the medical practice. These resources meet the needs of individuals who have more experience in the field, who seek specialized knowl-edge in a particular area of medical practice management, and/or who are completing preparations for the ACMPE board certification examinations.

■ Core Learning Series: Resources to become board certified

Board certification and Fellowship in ACMPE are well-earned badges of professional achievement. The designations Certified Medical Practice Executive (CMPE) and Fellow in ACMPE (FACMPE) indicate that the professional has attained significant levels of expertise across the full range of the medical practice administrator's responsibilities. The Medical Practice Management Core Learning Series is MGMA's recommended learning system for certification preparation. With attainment of the CMPE designation, practice executives will be well positioned to excel in their careers through ACMPE Fellowship.

Preface

HUMAN RESOURCE MANAGEMENT, formerly known as personnel management, is part of every medical practice executive's responsibilities. Although small medical practices generally do not have a human resources department, as a practice grows in complexity and size, it often develops a function or department to provide human resource management. Human resource management is committed to making sure that the right number of people with the appropriate skills are in place to accomplish the medical practice's goals and objectives.

Maintaining an efficient and effective human resources function is one of the most important tasks of a medical practice executive. The medical practice has to care for its staff and attract and retain the best employees. The human resources function of managing employees and addressing their needs and wants is a constant challenge. However, a function that exclusively focuses on the employees without an organizational commitment to increase patient satisfaction through a cultural change will ultimately fall short on improving service. A well-run medical practice with a strong vision, mission, goals, and objectives will use its human resource function to develop, implement, and maintain excellent programs in salary and wage administration, benefits administration, procedures and policies, recruitment, appraisal and evaluation, employee relations, training and development, and reward and recognition. The key to that success will be grounded in excellent service and quality patient care.

Human resources must therefore focus its commitment to a service culture that brings physicians and employees together to improve patient, physician, and employee satisfaction. A commitment focused on service to people (patients, employees, physicians) fosters a transformation to service excellence. The medical practice that focuses its effort on excellent service will differentiate itself from the competition. The human resources function can help facilitate the accountability of that service from physicians, administrators, and staff. The shared commitment and cooperation of these groups is critical for a culture of service to evolve meaningfully and to make a difference.

The purpose of this volume is to offer a set of resources to promote ideas regarding the human resources function and to help the medical practice executive better understand the elements and components of human resources.

Learning Objectives

AFTER READING THIS VOLUME, the medical practice executive will be able to:

1. Interpret and integrate federal, state, and local laws as well as industry human resources (HR) regulations into organizational policies and procedures;

2. Develop HR measurement and monitoring systems;

3. Explain the pros and cons of different compensation models and obtaining physician buy-in;

4. Give and receive feedback to improve individual and organizational performance;

5. Analyze the cost/benefit trade-offs of HR practices and the financial impacts on the practice;

6. Negotiate employee relations matters fairly to prevent labor disagreements and to ensure the safety of practice personnel;

7. Tolerate and understand the stress, criticism, and conflict related to HR matters, including disciplinary issues;

8. Identify core competencies and job responsibilities specific to medical services and create clear job descriptions;

9. Design recruitment and selection processes to ensure new personnel match position and staffing needs in the practice as well as strategic plans;

10. Understand the basis for physician behavior and deal with it effectively;

11. Assess and respond to staff needs for training and coaching; and

12. Monitor the practice's pay policies and update them with today's dynamic and diverse labor and industry trends and medical practice goals.

XYZ Medical Group

A LARGE MEDICAL GROUP recently acquired a small physician practice, XYZ Medical Group, with two physicians and eight employees. The practice lacked many of the basic elements of a human resources (HR) program. Employees had no position descriptions, no benefits, and never had formal written evaluations. Consistent disciplinary action was nonexistent. Staff knowledge on basic HR compliance issues was fraught with hearsay, past practice, and outdated information. The two physicians never sought professional help to develop any HR systems or processes. Now, being part of a larger medical group with a well-defined HR management system, a unique opportunity exists for the physicians and staff to learn and master a system that has proven effective.

During its 10 years of practice, XYZ Medical Group had never given a formal written evaluation to any employee. Wages were never tied to performance, and poor performances never received constructive feedback. The lack of written job descriptions led to infighting for the job duties everyone wanted to perform and inattention to the job functions no one wanted to do. In addition, merit pay did not exist, and pay increases were based on arbitrary time frames and nonmeasurable criteria.

The human resources department of the medical group that acquired this small practice tasked its assistant HR manager, Anne Baxter, with the responsibility to "teach the HR ropes" to XYZ's manager, Chris Dolan. Anne's first task was to introduce Chris to measures that would bring XYZ into line with the existing group's HR policies. In addition, XYZ had to be brought into compliance with the human resource management systems that were current for the medical practice industry.

Chris's first assignment was to put in place an employee handbook that described the employee benefits program and the evaluation process and schedule. Chris implemented a plan for formal written evaluations to occur at least once a year, which were initially scheduled to be conducted at the end of a calendar year and tied to the practice's operational goals, objectives, and financial objectives.

Staff members were evaluated by their supervisors, some of whom were physicians. Each employee reviewed the evaluation in advance so there were no surprises and the format and form used for evaluation was consistent for all employees. The position description and form is now used by the employee to ensure that the employee meets or exceeds his or her job requirements.

The practice, which had lacked many of the basic elements of an HR program, now had executed employee position descriptions, benefits, and a process for formal written evaluations. Wages were now tied to performance, and poor performers received constructive and consistent feedback. Staff knowledge on basic HR compliance issues was brought up to date through a series of in-service luncheons and the physicians embraced several unique opportunities to learn and master a system that has since proven effective.

Human Resource Management and the General Competencies

THE HUMAN RESOURCES DOMAIN within the *ACMPE Guide to the Body of Knowledge for Medical Practice Management* requires all five general competencies – (1) Professionalism, (2) Leadership, (3) Communication Skills, (4) Organizational and Analytical skills, and (5) Technical/ Professional Knowledge and Skills – to be in place for a medical practice executive to be successful.

■ Professionalism

The general competency of professionalism is key in the Human Resources domain. Human resources involve people in all walks of life who require an environment of continuous learning and assessment. The staff requires a constant flow of information, data, and resources to successfully perform its responsibilities. This information helps to set the foundation from which the staff can operate. A core set of procedures, policies, and practices forms the framework to guide the staff. The professionalism of how that information is managed, administered, and carried out sets the culture of the medical practice. The issues of "fairness, consistency, equity, legality, justice, morality, and ethics" all get rolled up into how professional the organization is in handling its people. A medical practice can have a great set of HR policies and procedures, but if they aren't administered and managed professionally, the practice suffers from a perceived lack of integrity and respect. Professionalism should be a core value for all medical practices, woven into the fabric of the organization. This commitment to professional standards allows the organization to carry out its human resources skills in the most effective manner.

■ Leadership

In the book *The 21 Irrefutable Laws of Leadership*, John Maxwell defines leadership as "influence – nothing more, nothing less."[1] He looks at leadership as the ability to influence other people, and recognizes that one is not capable of being an effective leader without integrity and trustworthiness. Stephen Covey sees the difference between management and leadership thusly: "Management is efficiency in climbing the ladder of success; leadership determines whether the ladder is leaning against the right wall."[2] With this in mind, the Human Resources domain requires the medical practice executive to lead an environment that fosters teamwork, accountability, and cooperation. It means that the physicians must work to develop an effective process of governance through education, training, and problem solving, and the leadership must support the organization toward its vision and the implementation of that vision. The Human Resources domain requires the leadership of the physicians and staff to support the recruitment, retention, and development of its employees to work toward improving patient care. That leadership is essential to develop the relationships needed to support excellent staff.

■ Communication Skills

Communication is the art and science of expressing and exchanging ideas in speech or writing. The intricacies of life require that the medical practice executive master both oral and written communication skills. In the Human Resources domain, communication is key to all parties – the person delivering the communication as well as the person receiving it. It is not uncommon for a human resources message to get misinterpreted or misunderstood due to lack of clear communication skills. Sometimes information is not organized logically, or emotion takes hold of a situation so that clear, objective information is not shared among physicians, staff, and patients. The challenges in the Human Resources domain are to identify the most appropriate communication vehicles for the identified audience and to support whatever dialogue needs to occur to answer questions, seek clarity, and resolve conflict.

■ Organizational and Analytical Skills

Appropriate management of the Human Resources domain involves a tremendous amount of data. Whether it is the determination of pay grades or salary and wage studies, developing a cost/benefit analysis of a benefit package, or evaluating the value of a continuing-education program, this domain demands an orientation to organizational and analytical skills.

The largest single line item on a financial statement usually involves the salaries and benefits of personnel. Knowing how to manage this line item requires an orientation to collecting and analyzing relevant information from multiple sources, discerning the salient data, and making sound decisions. The Human Resources domain requires the practice executive to interact with people, but the communication cannot be effective without solid organizational and analytical skills. These skills help the executive to manage practice resources and work toward achieving consensus regarding best performance.

■ Technical/Professional Knowledge and Skills

Running a medical practice requires a special set of technical and professional knowledge and skills unlike those for any other profession. The diversity and variety of situations that occur in a medical practice make its management unique. A medical practice executive is expected to have a general knowledge of many areas along with a capacity to handle detailed information in many specific areas. An example is a practice executive facilitating a physician board meeting, in which the board reviews the monthly and year-to-date financials, considers a marketing campaign for development of a new service, explores better risk management alternatives through consideration of changing to another malpractice carrier, assesses the progress made in the electronic health record (EHR) project, explores a clinical operation issue, nominates a new board member, hears the Ethics Committee's recommendation on a patient issue, and evaluates pension plan changes. These topics cover the broad spectrum of medical practice tasks and situations, requiring the medical executive to understand and apply principles of all eight performance domains: Financial Management, Human Resource Management, Planning and Marketing, Information Management, Risk Management, Governance and Organizational Dynamics, Business and Clinical Operations, and Professional Responsibility.

■ Summary

The medical practice executive is required to be proficient and competent in the five general competencies of Professionalism, Leadership, Communications, Organizational and Analytical Skills, and Technical/Professional Knowledge. The knowledge and skills needed in the Human Resources domain are critical for the success of both the practice executive and the medical practice. By learning this domain, the practice executive will be able to gain the skills needed to effectively lead the organization toward success.

Current Human Resource Management Issues

THE HUMAN RESOURCES PROFESSION is at a crossroads and needs to face up to its challenges or become a marginal contributor to organizational success. The medical practice executive is expected to substantially change the mix of activities in human resources to contribute to organizational strategy and effectiveness. The practice executive is challenged, however, with the wide mix of issues in the Human Resources domain.

Medical practices are constantly faced with issues to cut costs as managed-care companies and government insurers reduce reimbursement and external groups (e.g., malpractice insurers, vendors) increase costs for services provided. Cost-cutting measures typically fall between reducing staff wages and benefits or improving efficiencies in systems and processes so additional staff don't need to be hired. The Human Resources domain focuses on recruiting qualified people, providing competitive wages and benefits, training and educating, team building, managing performance, maintaining a positive work environment, supporting legal business practices and worker conditions, and carrying out the best HR strategy for the future.

Some of the expected HR trends and their resultant challenges in the market include:

- Technical and professional employee needs are increasing as work becomes more technology-oriented, and nontechnical employee jobs are also being impacted by technological advances. As "baby boomers" (those born between 1946 and 1964) continue to retire in the near future, the unavailability of skilled workers will intensify. A consequence is that the professional concerned with human resources will need to come up with creative ways to recruit qualified people and will need to be more proactive with succession planning.

- The training of nontechnical employees will shift to employers in the form of on-the-job training, as lower educational standards produce graduates unprepared for work. (Employers may even have to help with such basic skills as reading, writing, and arithmetic.)

- The lack of loyalty shown by both the employer and employee is changing the work culture. The labor force will be more transient, and staff members are likely to leave one job for another for a slight increase in pay. In addition, the employer's bottom-line approach will lead to more layoffs than ever before. The HR professional will therefore need to be more flexible and creative in workforce needs.

- Medical practices will have a greater demand to be customer-focused and require that employees have service and teamwork skills and be empowered to solve problems quickly.

- HR professionals will need a workforce with strong "soft" skills, such as a positive attitude, motivation, adaptability, and energy; and will be challenged to develop selection methods that evaluate these criteria. The HR focus will be on the whole employee, including training, counseling, and coaching.

- Outsourcing of staff and services will continue to be considered and will create conflicts with labor unions and loyal employees, who see this strategy as a threat to future jobs.

- As performance and outcomes become the "bottom line," HR professionals will need to develop effective performance management systems.

- As resources become scarce, new models for employment will need to be developed with the public and private sector, including job sharing, loaned employees, outsourced employees, and other collaborative models.

- Labor unions' traditional practices are becoming outdated in today's market, and have resulted in a decline in union memberships. Unions will require new approaches with management to address more beneficial solutions.

The executive concerned with HR in the future will not only focus on payroll and benefit administration, but provide opportunities to employees to customize service, including skill-building training, personalized coaching, resources for more effective problem solving, and better and simpler ways to track information. A clear understanding and knowledge of the Human Resources domain by the medical practice executive is needed to ensure the success of the medical practice.

Knowledge Needs

THE KNOWLEDGE BASE required to perform human resource management functions is comprehensive, incorporating the fields of finance, law, management, and information technology. This domain's published literature is as varied as it is complex, from rightsizing the medical practice to preparing manuals on job descriptions and personnel policies. Some of the literature is unique to medical practices, whereas other literature draws from the plethora of resources in manufacturing and the service industry. The need for advice and help in the Human Resources domain continues to grow as practice executives confront issues unique to them in the 21st century and seek answers to their complex problems.

The medical practice executive should perform both simple and complex management skills to promote employee productivity and organizational performance. The medical practice executive should:

- Understand federal and state employment laws by accurately recording and reporting compliance with regulations;

- Have knowledge of compensation and benefits administration to manage a program that best meets practice needs;

- Collect and analyze data on personnel issues and resolve the identified matters;

- Maintain currency on HR issues pertaining to employment, staffing, compensation, and regulations;

- Educate staff on best HR practices, including employee development, training, education, and communication;

- Advise management on personnel issues, including disciplinary action, labor disputes, employee morale, and consistent administration of personnel policies; and

- Use appropriate management information system (MIS) software to gather, analyze, and present HR data.

Demonstrating mastery of the Human Resources domain outlined within the *ACMPE Guide* requires the medical practice executive to understand the balance between management and employees and to make sure that all needs are met in the areas of administration, recruitment, compensation and benefits, training and development, health and safety, and employee relations. Formal education in human resources can lead to an associate's, bachelor's, master's, or doctoral degree. Course work includes instruction in personnel and organization policy, labor relations, labor law and regulations, motivation and compensation, career management, employee testing and assessment, recruitment and selection, employee- and job-training programs, and management of human resources programs and operations, among others. In addition, special certifications offered through the Society for Human Resource Management validate a person's knowledge in a particular human resources area. The medical practice executive may choose to pursue a self-directed course of study in human resources instead of seeking a formal degree or certification.

Many medical practice executives have staff that perform the human resources function and will therefore need to provide executive oversight and direction rather than directly running the functions. Choosing the right people for these leadership roles is critical and requires the medical practice executive to have a thorough understanding of the Human Resources domain. The executive needs to ensure that the HR department accurately represents and promotes the vision and values of the organization through its practices, and that it is approachable and credible and seen as a resource for all employees. The medical practice executive therefore has the responsibility for a successfully run HR department, primarily to:

- Develop HR policies and programs for the organization;

- Recommend employee relations practices to establish positive relationships;

- Address legal requirements and regulations;

- Establish wage and salary structures; pay policies; and performance, benefit, and safety and health programs;

- Establish recruitment and placement practices; and

- Develop training programs.

A medical practice executive who is knowledgeable in the Human Resources domain through mastery of essential skills allows for a positive environment of increased participation, higher morale, enhanced employee engagement, and improved team performance. Human resource management serves both a supportive function and one of leading strategy and effective change. The medical practice executive learns the Human Resources domain and its necessary skills and knowledge through formal education, self-directed learning, and experience in the field, all combining to achieve competence in the domain. Although exclusive self-directed learning can be pursued to master the domain, experience helps to solidify the knowledge, along with educational programs and workshops.

Overview of Human Resource Management Tasks

MEDICAL PRACTICE EXECUTIVES should develop and use their knowledge and skills to ensure that the following tasks related to human resource management are carried out:

■ TASK 1: **Design compensation and benefits programs consistent with the values of the organization**

This task develops an understanding of the various parts of compensation and benefits programs and how these programs must align with the organization's mission.

■ TASK 2: **Establish job classification systems**

This task introduces the components and factors necessary to develop a system to classify jobs. This system affords a better understanding of the dynamics necessary to lead a workforce that meets marketplace demands.

■ TASK 3: **Develop employee placement programs and facilitate workforce planning**

This task involves the key aspects of understanding employee placement programs and developing workforce planning efforts.

■ TASK 4: **Establish employee appraisal and evaluation systems**

This task involves the ability to explain key job responsibilities to employees as well as the core competencies needed for medical practice positions and how they are incorporated into job descriptions.

■ TASK 5: **Develop and implement employee training programs**

This task relates to the key issues of employee training programs and how these programs will address staff competence and the proficiencies needed to perform the key job functions.

■ TASK 6: **Establish employee relations and conflict resolution programs**

This task identifies the programs and resources available to help the employee and management resolve issues that prevent successful accomplishment of the organization's goals and objectives.

■ TASK 7: **Maintain compliance with employment laws**

This task addresses the numerous laws and regulations regarding employee relations and their application to the employee. Understanding and embracing these laws will help to ensure that staff members are treated fairly as well as to mitigate risk for employment-related lawsuits.

Design Compensation and Benefits Programs Consistent with the Values of the Organization

HUMAN RESOURCES MANAGEMENT should be closely aligned with the vision, mission, goals, and objectives of the medical practice. It is through the employees that these goals are accomplished, so it is important that the employees are highly satisfied and committed to achieving the organizational goals – in particular, financial success and high patient satisfaction. A well-trained workforce with high employee satisfaction and low employee turnover usually results in excellent outcomes. Low employee turnover leads to reduced expenses to recruit and train staff.

■ Mission of the Medical Practice

The medical practice needs to have an organizational philosophy and/or mission shared with its employees so that there is a common understanding of the organization's overreaching mission. In addition, sharing of its values provides a set of common understandings by which action is organized. The medical practice's values help to shape employee behavior to accomplish the medical practice's mission.

The mission and financial goals of the practice dictate the pay and benefits for the employees. Medical practices should decide where they want to fall within benchmarked data derived from other medical practices in terms of pay and benefits. One that sets its pay below the 50th percentile of the market will not be able to recruit qualified people without some offsetting benefits for an employee to consider. For example, although pay may be lower, the benefit structure may be more flexible (flex dollars to use toward either health, dental, or life insurance), the work environment may be more open to innovation and creativity (flexible hours or telecommuting opportunities), or the mission of the group is compelling (caring for unmet needs of the poor and underserved).

Some medical groups provide an annual employee pay/benefit report to each employee that shows the value of his or her job in areas outside of paid compensation. The personalized statement provides a total compensation package that shows the combined value of annualized pay and benefits (salary + paid time off + employer-paid taxes + employer-paid benefits such as health, life, dental, vision, disability, retirement, and so forth). This type of report can often be a strong employee motivator.

■ Basic Compensation

Compensation must be fair, equitable, and related to the job tasks that the person is expected to perform. An employee may initially be paid based on his or her skill, knowledge, or competency-based expertise. The higher the employee's skill or competency, the higher his or her pay. For example, a manager with a bachelor's degree is usually paid less than someone with a master's degree.

If an incentive program is developed, it should be fair, consistent, and measurable. The criteria should easily be understood and be able to be tracked. A performance-based compensation model is the most common type of compensation model provided to employees. It is based on merit and is easy to develop, track, and administer. An employee is hired at a salaried or hourly wage and provided wage increases based on how well he or she performed in a previous period. Incentive pay options allow the employee to receive a bonus based on completing pre-determined job goals. If the goals aren't achieved, the employee doesn't receive an increase in pay. For example, a medical group may decide that an average performer receives a 3 percent increase and an exceptional performer receives a 4 percent increase. A determination of the difference between average and high performers is needed for such merit increases.

Physician Compensation

A way in which a medical practice compensates its physicians for services provided is one of the most important issues affecting a medical group, and can ultimately determine the success or failure of the practice. A physician may be paid based on knowledge or skill. A physician with dual-board certification may be paid more than a physician without that certification. A cardiologist may be paid more than a pediatrician, based on the cardiologist's skill, job knowledge, and additional years of training. In addition, a physician may be provided with a fixed salary based on anticipated work with a formula for a bonus or incentive if the workload is exceeded.

Physician compensation will reflect a medical practice's mix of physicians and its legal and cost structure, along with its culture, history, and external influences. Regardless of the plan, the compensation method must reflect the medical practice's goals. It must reward productivity that is consistent with the mission and values of the organization. It must be fair and consistently administered, simple and easily understood, and comply with the law. It should be aligned with the financial needs of the organization and allow the medical group to retain current providers and recruit new providers. Above all, the plan must be fair.[3]

Staff Compensation

The medical practice executive should routinely evaluate position compensation based on internal and external factors, evaluating the initial pay offered an employee and the merit increases that an employee receives over time. Adjustments in pay tables and ranges should occur at the same time each year to allow for a consistent process and approach unless there are some extenuating circumstances. Pay adjustments should be communicated to employees in writing, including the reason for the adjustment. A poorly run program may allow inconsistencies to enter a system, thus creating unintentional pay inequities.

The marketplace needs to be considered when developing compensation scales (see discussion of job importance in Task 2). The marketplace must always be considered in recruiting well-qualified employees and to keep employee turnover low. In addition, an economic condition, such as a period of inflation or recession, will impact the kinds of pay scales that are offered to employees.

The local market may require a medical practice to take a different approach from national or regional approaches. A medical practice located in a rural or urban area may need to offer a higher rate of pay or other incentives to encourage a person to join the practice. A potential employee needs to see that the higher compensation or benefits are worth the potential change in quality of life.

A practice may need to recruit outside of its local area due to shortages in a certain type of position. A tougher labor market to recruit a particular position will result in a medical group having to pay a higher market rate for that position. For example, a pharmacist shortage may require the medical practice to seek candidates from nearby metropolitan areas or even pursue a national search. These commitments become very expensive recruiting efforts and require additional recruiting support to deal with new issues of travel costs, introduction to the community, costs of a real estate agent, housing relocation expenses, and other transition costs.

The medical practice executive should evaluate pay scales periodically to ensure that there is parity within the pay grades. Sometimes a position within the marketplace changes and requires a modification of pay. When new hires are brought into the organization at a higher rate of pay than traditional, internal parity needs to be made for other comparable positions within the organization to ensure equitable pay.

Job-Driven Compensation

How compensation scales are developed determines how successful the medical group is in attracting and retaining employees. Difficult-to-recruit positions, such as certified coders and nuclear medicine technologists, may have special or higher pay scales. Some positions may require a higher-than-average starting salary to be competitive in the marketplace.

Some positions are difficult to recruit due to intense external competitiveness. There may be a shortage of qualified candidates for a certain position in the local market due to few if any formal training programs or an increase in need due to a growing industry. For example, nurses are difficult to recruit because there are so many groups trying to recruit the same labor pool – from hospitals, nursing homes, and home care agencies, to schools, medical groups, and public health agencies. This external competitiveness will lead organizations to consider paying nurses at higher rates or deciding to run a practice with staff that has lower skills levels (e.g., medical assistants).

Certain positions may even warrant a medical practice to offer a sign-on bonus for difficult-to-fill positions. With shortages in nurses, radiology technologists, professional coders, and other competitive positions, other options may be retention bonuses given to the employee after staying on the job for a 6- or 12-month period.

Recruitment packages need to be sensitive to the current workforce and current staffing. If co-workers see that tremendous resources are placed on recruiting additional staff, but no resources are devoted to retain current employees, there may be perceived inequity issues, which may prompt certain employees to leave the medical practice and thus create a larger recruitment issue for the practice.

In addition, wage compression can occur wherein all the positions in a like category make similar wages due to the labor market. For example, all professional coders may make a similar wage regardless of experience because most of the coders are being paid toward the top of the compensation range. This compression makes it difficult to manage ongoing resources for other employees who may expect the same type of plan for themselves.

Pay Grades/Steps

Published salary surveys use data from internal and external sources to develop a tool that can be invaluable to a medical group to know the financial factors to consider regarding employee compensation. Such tools include salary groups and pay scales within each salary group. Professional associations such as MGMA print benchmarked salary data for physicians, and some state MGMA groups publish benchmark data on staff. In addition, the federal government publishes national data on certain positions that can help a medical practice determine the kind of pay scale it wants to have for a particular position. These updated data help the medical practice executive determine if the practice's ranges need to be adjusted to reflect changing market rates.

Salary survey data in addition to job structure within the organization are used to develop pay grades and ranges for positions within the medical group. Salary grades group like jobs together with the same pay grade and pay rate. The number of salary grades is determined by the medical group based on the types and number of positions within the practice. Salary grades have a minimum, midpoint, and maximum for each pay grade and have some overlap among other pay grades to allow for differences in employee experience levels in different ranges. For example, a newly hired employee in pay grade 24 may make less than a highly experienced employee in pay grade 23. A compensation strategy that develops fewer and broader pay grades simplifies pay grade structure and allows employees to achieve higher pay in the same range.

The development of salary-increase guides helps to establish clear expectations and allows for better budgeting. If a practice usually has half of the employees receiving a 3 percent increase and half receiving a 4 percent increase, then the administrator can budget the maximum amount of money that will be allocated to salary increases for the next fiscal year.

Pay grades can have a maximum pay scale so that an employee may hit the top of the range. Organizations need to determine if the person is "redlined" so that he or she is not eligible for any pay increases or whether there is a special incentive program available to senior employees.

Informal Salary Information Sources

Informal salary surveys allow the organization to respond to changing market forces. During the recruitment process, HR professionals glean large amounts of information from candidates including salary and benefits data. If potential candidates will not work for a medical group because of "low pay," this kind of information should be revealed during the interview process. Also, new hires may validate the competitive pay and benefits of the employer when they sign up for their benefits in the new organization. Data from these types of encounters can be invaluable for the organization.

In addition, peers can share data about why employees are leaving a certain organization, and exit interviews can provide other anecdotal information about an employee's personal experience. For example, an employee may share that he is leaving the medical group to work at a competitor's organization in the same job for a one-dollar-an-hour increase in pay. However, all the factors would need to be considered. In this case, at the competitor's office, the employee would receive an additional $2,080 in annual salary ($1 x 2,080 full-time hours worked per year), but he would also have to pay $3,000 out-of-pocket for benefits. The net effect would be a salary loss of $920 due to increased benefits costs. This result suggests that the employee might have additional or unstated reasons for leaving the organization.

Confidentiality of Compensation Data

The medical group needs to determine what types of compensation/pay information can be shared with employees and what information should remain private. For example, a group may elect to keep salaries private, but communicate the bonus structure with everyone, telling staff and physicians that is was calculated based on seniority, pay grade, or other factors. Private information is, obviously, private and confidential. It should not be shared with other people and should remain protected information in the employee file.

A medical practice should have a policy on what type of pay information is shared. A closed policy is one that does not openly share pay grades or ranges. For example, a position is posted and the pay grade is 23, which means that the position's minimum pay is $12 per hour and maximum pay is $16 per hour. This open policy allows the employee to know whether he or she is interested in this position or not. A closed policy would not post a pay grade, may not openly share that information, and would share pay information only to a final candidate being considered. Knowing whether to share certain kinds of pay information helps the medical practice executive to focus on following its policies.

Sharing such data can create conflict and tension. However, certain groups, such as government agencies, share salary information openly, and this is a common expectation for this group. Overall, salary information should be kept confidential and staff should be encouraged to maintain confidentiality regarding salaries.

■ Formal Benefits

Whereas an employee's direct pay is easily seen, the indirect pay, consisting of the employee's benefits, retirement benefits, and social security, is often overlooked. Formal benefits may include medical, dental, and vision plans, short- and long-term disability insurance, life insurance, pension plan, savings and investment plans, unemployment insurance, and workers' compensation premiums, among others. These benefits usually have a shared cost between the employer and employee based on a certain percentage. In larger organizations, the pay/benefit mix in total compensation could be 20 percent of the employee's wages. For example, an employee making $30,000 per year could expect to receive approximately $6,000 in additional benefits from the organization.

A flexible benefit plan allows the employee to choose from a range of benefits that best meet his/her current needs. There may be a dollar-amount cap to apply to those benefits. For example, one employee may have a $1,500 cap that is applied to a $1,000 medical premium and a $500 vision premium, and another employee may apply his or her $1,500 to a $750 dental premium and $750 toward a medical premium.

Benchmarking data helps the employer determine if the benefit package being offered to employees is competitive within the marketplace. If the market shows that employers generally provide benefits up to 20 percent of the employee payroll, and a particular employer provides only 10 percent, that factor may influence whether an employee will join the organization.

Benefits have short- and long-term effects on the employee base. A practice may decide to fund a certain benefit today, but regret its financial impact on the group in the future. As an example, in the past, the automobile industry decided to fully fund retiree health premiums when costs were well within control and there were few retirees. However, with an aging workforce and retirees living longer, the financial impact has become cost prohibitive, prompting the industry to decide how to handle benefits for the future. These lessons learned can help medical groups design benefit packages that are fair, equitable, and affordable for both the employee and employer.

Goal-Driven Benefits

Equity Ownership

Equity ownership may allow a physician to participate in owning a part of the medical practice, which would allow the physician to participate in any financial gains. In for-profit organizations that allow stock to be purchased, an employee can purchase stock in the company and have equity ownership. On the downside, equity ownership also means sharing losses.

Some medical groups have shareholders and nonshareholders. Compensation methods will be different for the two groups. For example, depending on the legal structure, a physician may have stock options or direct ownership in a medical group. This arrangement will impact how the physician is paid.

Profit Sharing

A medical group may decide to offer its employees the opportunity to participate in a profit-sharing program that provides employees with additional pay if the medical group meets or exceeds its financial goals. The challenge is to decide how much of the profit will be distributed and to whom. Or, bonuses may be provided if the practice meets its financial goals.

As an incentive to achieve department goals, a medical practice may decide to provide a team reward if the team achieves a certain financial outcome. For example, a medical group with an urgent care center may provide an incentive for a team to see more than 50 patients a day. This goal would mean the team would be required to get all the patients through the center on a timely basis and avoid any walk-outs from the clinic due to timeliness issues.

Gainsharing

Gainsharing is a process by which employees are involved in performance enhancements and share the financial benefits of these improvements made by the medical practice. Gainsharing is a common practice among Fortune 500 companies. Unlike bonuses that are provided annually, gainsharing allows regular financial payments to be made to the employee, such as on a monthly or quarterly basis. The system instills immediate understanding by the employee on what is needed to be accomplished to achieve a gainsharing bonus. Although the system may be incomplete on providing incentives to employees to achieve all organizational goals, this tool has been used for many companies to achieve phenomenal results.

Insurance Benefits

The types of insurance that may be offered usually apply to health or life.

Health Insurance

With more than 40 million people in the United States currently lacking health insurance,[4] and many Americans believing health care is a basic right, access to health insurance coverage is a key benefit for a medical practice. Employees may seek employment based on whether the employer offers health insurance. It is common for smaller medical practices not to offer health insurance to their employees, but most larger practices have to offer health insurance to competitively recruit employees.

Some medical groups contract with external groups to handle their health insurance coverage. Other medical practices may cover their own health insurance through a self-insured plan. Regardless of the arrangement, health insurance must be managed effectively and efficiently, with cost containment being one of the largest issues plaguing the medical practice today.

In addition to basic health insurance, additional specific health-related insurance may include the following:

- *Dental, Vision, and Hearing Insurance.* Dental and/or vision insurance offerings can be employer- and/or employee-funded and offer coverage under health maintenance organization (HMO), preferred provider organization (PPO), or traditional plans. Hearing and vision insurance may be options for those employees and/or dependents who experience hearing and/or vision problems.

- *In-House Medical Services.* As an employee benefit, medical practices may offer access to certain types of medical services within the organization. Services may range from free access to physician services to reduced fees for pharmaceuticals and medical supplies.

- *Travel Insurance.* For medical practices that require employees to travel to different locations for business, offering travel insurance in case of problems is a common, and inexpensive, benefit.

- *Long-Term and Short-Term Disability Insurance.* Short-term disability coverage defines plan days covered, plan funding, and what is and is not considered a short-term disability. Plans that allow pregnancy as a short-term disability are very popular for employers with a potentially child-bearing workforce.

- *Post-Retirement Medical Benefits.* With continued concerns about access to health insurance, some medical groups offer employees access to medical benefits after retirement. Whereas access to medical benefits through the Consolidated Omnibus Budget Reconciliation Act of 1985 (COBRA) are offered for up to 18 months after an employee leaves an organization, post-retirement medical benefits are offered only to those employees who officially retire. Qualified retirees may need to meet certain age requirements, and payment of medical benefits may be based on years of service at the organization prior to retiring.

- *Long-Term Care Plans.* As the population continues to age, long-term care plans are becoming more popular. For an employee/employer contribution, the plan covers the cost for a certain percentage of care provided in an approved long-term care facility.

Life Insurance

Life insurance may be just for the employee, or the practice may offer a plan for the employee and dependents. The plan will have limits usually based on the employee's income or a percentage of his income. In addition to life insurance policies that cover general death benefits, some employers offer an additional coverage for accidental death, such as due to automobile accident, plane crash, or similar accident.

Retirement and Severance Benefits

Pension Plans

Pension plans allow the employee to have money available for retirement. The pension plan may be fully funded by the employer or may have joint employer and employee contributions.

Severance Pay

As more organizations are downsizing, going bankrupt, or going through mergers, acquisitions, and consolidations, they have developed a severance pay policy for employees whose positions are eliminated. Usually, these policies are based on the employees' employment status (full vs. part-time), the employee's class (exempt vs. nonexempt employee, management vs. executive), and years of service (less than 1 year, 1 to 5 years, 5+ years). These differentiations will determine the level of severance provided to an employee.

■ Issues Related to Benefits

Benefit Cost Sharing

Employers determine which benefits are employer-paid, which are employee-paid, and which are shared by both the employer and employee. Inflation, malpractice premium increases, and reduced reimbursement from managed care plans, among other factors, are affecting the bottom line of many practices. Therefore, the employee is picking up more of the cost of benefits. The employer must be careful with this strategy, though, because it may lead to higher turnover and a medical practice that is less effective in the marketplace. Although this shift in payment responsibility may be a cost-effective approach for the employer, it may strap the employee with higher costs and a perceived drop in quality of life, leading to employee dissatisfaction.

A medical practice may choose to be self-funding for a certain part of its benefit costs. For example, it may contract out its life insurance and short-term disability benefits, but self-fund its health insurance costs through its own insurance plan or medical malpractice through an offshore captive insurance company.

Eligibility

Benefit plans can be established for certain types of employee types and classes of employees. A medical practice can define the difference between full-time and part-time employment for benefit purposes. A full-time position may be 36+ hours of work per week, which allows the employee to participate in the full-time benefit plan, whereas part-time benefits would be available for employees working from 20 to 35 hours a week. Those employees who work less than 20 hours each week could be considered ineligible for benefits. More benefits would be available for the full-time employee as an incentive to work full time. Examples would be that a full-time employee would receive reduced premiums on health insurance and an employer-paid short-term disability benefit, whereas a part-time employee would receive a higher medical premium and no short-term disability benefit.

Benefits could also vary based on job class so that the physician receives a different type of benefit structure than the staff. The benefit package, however, needs to be carefully designed with appropriate human resources and legal counsel to ensure that the plan meets federal and state legal requirements and doesn't violate any specific laws. For example, the medical practice may want to offer a pension plan to physicians and employees, but offer a shorter vesting period for physicians. That change in benefit may not be allowed based on how the practice and employees are organized. Legal counsel can review pension laws to determine what kinds of variables are allowed.

Legal and Tax Issues

Retirement plans can be qualified or nonqualified. Qualified plans do not discriminate among employees, are tax-exempt, and offer a tax deferral benefit for employee and employer contributions.

Qualified plans allow the medical practice a tax deduction for plan contributions wherein employees do not pay taxes on plan assets until they are distributed, and plan earnings are tax deferred. To maintain a qualified status, an employer must follow the requirements of the Internal Revenue Service (IRS), the Department of Labor, and the Employee Retirement Income Security Act of 1974 (ERISA).

A nonqualified plan has easy plan adoption and no coverage, eligibility, or participation requirements. It allows contributions beyond caps established for qualified plans. A medical practice can decide to provide nonqualified deferred compensation plans to only a select group of employees (e.g., physicians). Whereas a qualified plan must be written and must meet participation, vesting, and funding requirements, a nonqualified plan need not meet these requirements. A nonqualified plan allows the employee to get more compensation.

However, nonqualified plans have drawbacks. The medical practice won't claim a tax deduction for employee amounts until the employee receives that money as income, perhaps many years in the future. The employee may not receive the money at all, however, if the medical practice becomes insolvent, because that money is subject to the claims of the medical practice's creditors; in other words, it is unsecured.

Some benefits are legally required, such as payment of unemployment benefits, workers' compensation premiums, and taking out monies for federal, state, and local taxes. When designing a compensation and benefits program, the medical practice must be aware of the following laws and how they may impact the development of the plan.

ERISA

For the medical practice, ERISA is a federal law that sets minimum standards for voluntary established pension and health plans to protect plan participants. ERISA requires participants to be provided with information such as plan features and funding, participation standards, vesting, benefit accrual and funding, fiduciary responsibilities for assets, and a grievance and appeals process.

HIPAA

The Health Insurance Portability and Accountability Act of 1996 (HIPAA) was approved to amend the Internal Revenue Code of 1986. Its primary purpose is to improve portability and continuity of health insurance coverage, eliminate misuse in health insurance and its delivery, promote medical savings account use, improve access to long-term care services, and simplify health insurance administration.

COBRA

COBRA amends ERISA, the Internal Revenue Code, and Public Health Service Act to ensure the continuation of group health coverage that otherwise would have been terminated. It allows certain former employees and dependents to temporarily continue health coverage at group rates, which are usually less expensive than private health coverage. In general, the law applies to health plans with 20+ employees and requires that the plan have rules detailing how an individual becomes entitled to these benefits. Life insurance is not covered under COBRA.

Medical Practice Payroll Obligations

Every medical practice, as an employer, must report to the IRS with regard to the income paid to each employee. The medical practice should determine the amount of income tax to withhold. The medical practice, based on its size, will either deposit the taxes it withholds for future payment to the IRS, or will send it directly to the IRS. The three components of federal payroll taxes are federal income taxes withheld from the employee's wages, the employees' share of Federal Insurance Contributions Act (FICA) taxes, and the employer's matching share of FICA taxes.

FICA comprises a Medicare hospital insurance tax of 1.45 percent on all taxable wages and Old-Age, Survivors, and Disability Insurance (OASDI) of 6.2 percent (commonly called Social Security). Therefore, a medical practice must withhold 7.65 percent of each employee's wage and match this amount with its own funds.

In addition to these taxes, the medical practice may be liable to pay IRS Code Section 457 plans, workers' compensation insurance, and/or unemployment insurance.

Social Security

The Social Security Act is the law governing most operations of the Social Security program. The original Social Security Act was enacted in 1935 and subsequent amendments comprise 20 titles. The OASDI program is authorized by title II of the Social Security Act. Social Security is usually referred to as a "tax." It is actually the amount of contribution based on a percent of earnings, up to an annual maximum, that must be paid by employers and employees on wages from employment under FICA. Usually, medical practices withhold contributions from wages, add an equal amount of contributions, and pay both on a current basis.

IRS Code Section 457/Deferred Compensation

Section 457 plans are nonqualified, deferred compensation plans established by state or local government and tax-exempt employers. If a medical practice is considered to be a tax-exempt employer, it would qualify to provide this type of plan. The practice could establish either eligible or ineligible plans, which are subject to the specific requirements and deferral limitations of Section 457 of the IRS code.

Workers' Compensation

The concept of workers' compensation (generally known as "workers' comp") dates back almost 100 years, to 1908, when it was enacted for federal employees. It relates to the liability of the employer to pay damages for employee injuries incurred while the employee is on the job. Workers' compensation includes an elective schedule of compensation and provides a procedure to determine liability and compensation. It is actually an insurance program that pays an employee for medical and disability benefits for work-related injuries or certain diseases. If an employee is injured on the job, the employee's medical treatment costs are paid by the workers' compensation policy. If the employee has a job-related injury that prevents him/her from working, the employee will receive weekly income through the policy until able to return to work. Medical practices must either obtain coverage by purchasing a workers' compensation insurance policy or become licensed to "self-insure" by the state labor commissioner.

Unemployment Insurance

Unemployment compensation was created by the Social Security Act of 1935 to help eligible people who, through no fault of their own, are unemployed. Monetary benefits usually are determined according to the amount of former wages and/or weeks of work. The program is funded by employer taxes, either federal or state, and is a partnership between the federal and state governments wherein the program is based on federal law but administered by state employees under state law. Each state creates its own program within the guidelines of the federal government. The state statute develops the eligibility and disqualification provisions, benefit amount, state tax base, and state rate.

■ Other Benefits

Recruiting Bonuses

Employees may be provided with a "recruitment bonus" or "referral bonus" if a person is referred to the medical practice, accepts the position, and stays in the position for a certain period of time. This bonus generates employee buy-in of the recruitment process, creates awareness of difficult-to-recruit positions, and encourages employees to network with others to promote the organization for future employment.

Paid Time Off

An employee may be afforded time off if it does not conflict with the needs of the department and is pre-approved by a supervisor. Moreover, employers are currently moving to a flexible program of paid time off (PTO) that combines time off for sick leave, vacation, holidays, and jury duty into one pool. In this way, the employee manages one "bucket" of time instead of having different buckets of time. The PTO plan mitigates situations in which employees would dip into an unrelated bucket, such as an employee with a sick child who inappropriately draws on the "sick time" bucket because there is no time left in his or her vacation time bucket.

Financial Planning/Counseling

While medical practices may provide retirement resources for the employee through Social Security and a pension plan, those resources may not be enough for the employee at the time of retirement to maintain a certain quality of life. As a result, a voluntary investment plan such as a 401(k) plan would allow the employee to defer receiving compensation in order to have the amount contributed to the plan for future use at retirement. Information on Employee Assistance Programs (EAPs), including financial counseling, can be found in Task 7.

Housing Finance Assistance

Owning a house is an integral part of the "American dream," and organizations can help employees achieve that dream through offering housing finance assistance. An employee can benefit from housing finance assistance, including financial planning, exploration of options available, and reduced rates through group consortiums.

Child Care/Elder Care

Caring for family, such as children or elderly parents, is an important employee value. A medical practice that helps employees address these issues can be a strong employee satisfier. A medical practice may choose to offer a plan for the employee to save money pre-tax to pay for these services or may actually offer these services through the practice at a reduced employee rate.

Charitable Matching Contributions

Some medical practices offer a charitable matching program that matches a certain percentage of funds that an employee contributes to a charity. For example, if an employee contributes $100 to the American Red Cross, the employer might contribute 50 percent of the employee's contribution, or $50, to that agency too. Certain limitations may apply to this benefit, such as contribution caps and select charities.

IRAs

An Individual Retirement Account (IRA) allows the employee to invest pre-tax dollars in an investment plan that is managed by the employee. It is a self-directed, employee-funded retirement plan. Employers may choose to contribute money to this type of plan instead of managing their own pension plan.

Informal Benefits

Informal benefits, such as gift certificates or other tokens of appreciation, are discussed in Task 4.

TASK 2　**Establish Job Classification Systems**

WITHIN AN ORGANIZATION, every job has its own inherent value, serves a specific purpose and function, and helps the organization perform well to serve patients. Without an analysis and job assessment, it is difficult to determine how each position fits within the medical practice. There are numerous ways to assess a job. The components presented in this task address issues the medical practice executive should consider in conducting an analysis.

The human resources function supports the appropriate employment of the type and number of employees in addition to helping to retain well-qualified employees. In a small medical practice, the physician and/or medical practice manager are responsible for human resource duties. In larger practices, a human resources manager or department, usually under the direction of the medical practice executive, is responsible for these functions. Human resources serve a key role in employee orientation about the organization, training on the job, and education about certain issues such as HIPAA, compliance, and interviewing.

■ Job Importance

The relative worth of a job is usually determined by external forces and the marketplace. That worth places the position within a certain pay grade and category within a job table. For example, if a person supervises an activity or person, that is a critical aspect of a job. It requires a higher level of knowledge, experience, and background; and the position within the job table should recognize that supervision.

Some medical groups may modify the importance of a job within an organization depending on the organizational culture. A medical practice that performs medical research and wants to be the best in that field may choose to place a greater value and emphasis on that position than other medical groups do.

Decision making can be difficult on an objective basis. One tool to help the evaluator rate a position can be a point system. That system assigns points to certain aspects of a position. Those positions with more points are placed in a higher position grade than those positions with fewer points.

■ Position Analysis

Analyzing a position can take numerous forms. A medical practice executive or human resources professional should determine the most effective way to collect data. An interview with the employee or supervisor can help to determine the key functions and responsibilities. However, sometimes staff members are not good at describing all the facets of a job. The interview is a good start, but may not collect all the necessary data. Observation of the position is time-consuming and may not cover all aspects of the job over time. For example, a manager may observe the position during the day, but not during the evening when key job elements are performed. Another method to analyze a position is through a questionnaire whereby the person in the position completes a survey that allows him or her to enter comments and self-observations. A diary or time log that the employee completes individually allows the person to log the types of duties and functions performed over the course of the day or week. A log, however, is only as good as the person who completes it. Any and/or all of these methods can serve as a method to analyze a position.

The job analysis needs to evaluate the job activities. Certain activities are easy to evaluate, such as telephone answering, filing, charge entry, and administration of injections. Other job activities are difficult to analyze, such as negotiating a contract, solving problems within a task, and developing programs. The job analysis should be nonbiased, objective, and accurate in stating the true nature of the job over time. The job analysis should be performed continually to fully capture the position's duties, responsibilities, and skills.

Note that a person may be accountable for a function but actually not perform that function. For example, a nurse may be accountable for the proficiency and competency of the staff performing lab tests within the office, but the nurse does not personally perform a lab test within the office. Defining accountabilities helps to better define the job.

The analysis of the position allows it to be appropriately evaluated to determine the value of the position within the organization and how it fits with other positions within the organization. The position must also be evaluated under the Fair Labor Standards Act of 1938 (FLSA) to determine whether the job is eligible for overtime pay or can be exempted from the act and not paid overtime. The medical practice must be able to show that the position has been evaluated based on the work that is performed as described in the written job description.

■ Job Descriptions

Performance standards outline what is expected from each employee. A professional coder may be required to code 20 charts per hour, or a telephone triage nurse may be expected to handle up to 15 telephone calls per hour. Establishing the standards either in the position description (or a separate document) is important to allow for clear understanding of expectations.

Allowing an employee to help write the job description builds employee accountability and ownership of the position. It helps the employee to know the kinds of things that are included in a position description before it is finalized by the human resources professional.

A job description provides a general overview of the position being performed and has the following sections:

Position Title

A position title provides a description and expectation of the position being performed. The title of "nurse" conveys a common knowledge held by the general public of that person's job requirements and expertise. A common practice is for physicians' medical assistants to refer to themselves as "nurses." Overall, a position title should reflect community standards and help co-workers and the public to understand what that person does.

General Statement of Duties

A general statement of duties lists the primary duties of the position. This statement is a general summary of the position.

Supervision Received or Exercised

Listing the supervision received or exercised helps to define the authority level that the position has within the organization. Reporting to the CEO is a different level of supervision than reporting to a team lead. Also, supervising 50 people is very different from supervising one person.

Essential Functions

Essential functions list the key components of the job, usually in order of importance or frequency of use. This list usually includes a statement at the end of "other duties as assigned" to allow for flexibility in the position.

Educational Requirements

The education level guides the position's expectations. If a position requires a bachelor's degree, then a person with an associate's degree knows that he/she is not eligible for the position. If a position description requires a person to be a graduate of a medical assistant program, a state-tested nursing assistant knows that he or she is not eligible for the position. However, setting educational levels too high may restrict or limit certain people who may be well qualified for the position but lack the educational requirements.

Experience, Skills, Abilities, and Competencies

If a candidate needs a special skill, ability, or competency to fill a position, then those people lacking that ability are not qualified for the position. In the first example, the requirement of "past experience with a billing program" excludes those people who lack that background. A skill may supersede an educational requirement, such as "knowledge of Current Procedural Terminology CPT® [5] and International Classification of Diseases, Ninth Revision (ICD-9) codes," whereas an educational requirement might be an associate's degree in medical records. In a second example, if administering injections is an ability *required* for the job, a candidate who lacks that skill would not be considered for the job. In a third example, if knowledge of implementing Occupational Safety and Health Administration (OSHA) plans is *necessary*, an applicant who doesn't even know what OSHA stands for obviously would not be considered.

In another scenario, a nurse who has exclusively worked in a hospital oncology floor wants to work in a pediatric medical practice performing telephone triage. The job *requires* an RN degree and prior pediatric experience. Although it is possible, of course, for a nurse to become oriented and trained in a new area, the primary concern is whether the applicant's past experience offers any benefit to the future position. Also to be considered is whether it is worthwhile for the medical practice to spend the time, effort, and energy to orient a person to a new job if he/she lacks the basic core skills necessary in pediatrics (in this case, ambulatory vs. inpatient practice, adult vs. pediatric issues).

The fifth example involves hiring a radiology technologist (RT). The RT is *required* to take X-rays and *preferred* to have experience in phlebotomy (blood draws) to help the lab with blood draws during downtimes. In this situation, an applicant may have the technical skills for radiology, but lack the additional phlebotomy skills. This candidate's radiology skills are licensed and required, and the blood draw skills can be learned either through on-the-job training or pre-determined classes because the skill is *preferred* and not required, so this applicant is qualified for the position.

In the final example, if a candidate is seeking a position as transcriptionist and can type 80 words per minute but cannot transcribe medical terminology and has no experience in a clinical setting, then this applicant might be better suited for data entry or possible front-desk work.

However, when the job description states "preferred" rather than "required," the medical practice can consider others who lack that skill or ability. A person with a strong knowledge of CPT® codes, for example, may still be able to apply for a position if the educational requirement of a medical records degree is preferred, not required.

Therefore, each position should have a job description as well as a statement about the physical requirements of the job. Examples would be the ability to "sit for prolonged periods of time"; "work and move within departments of the medical practice"; "lift up to 50 pounds"; or " transfer information from paper to computer, from computer to computer, and to communicate in person and on the telephone"; or possessing "manual dexterity to operate computer and office machines (copier, fax)." This type of statement allows the supervisor and candidate to know what is expected from the successful job candidate and clearly communicates to the potential job candidate the physical requirements of the job. A candidate who cannot lift 50 pounds should not apply for a position that requires this skill.

A position description may also describe interactions with other types of positions. A file clerk may interact with the public in completing medical record releases, and with medical receptionists needing medical records. A compliance officer would interact with attorneys, physicians, and the practice administrator. These types of interactions also impact the level of skills and abilities needed for the position.[6]

Classification Scheme

Job classes help to provide structure within the job analysis. For example, a housekeeper and dietary clerk may be in the same job class, and a medical assistant and pharmacy technician may serve in another job class or family. Education, background, experience, and critical functions can determine job classes.

A *job task* is a high-level function describing a key component of a position. For example, a nurse may have the job task of providing telephone triage. The task doesn't refer to the types of telephone triage, but the overall high-level task.

Duties may be considered relatively easy, average workload, or highly complex. For example, filing lab results under the laboratory tab of the medical record may be considered as a relatively easy function, but filing and sorting research reports based on National Institutes of Health (NIH) funding criteria would be a more difficult filing job and a more complex duty. Duties should be differentiated, not to underemphasize the importance of certain job tasks, but to aid in position analysis.

Medical job categories help to place positions within certain groups. These groupings allow for better organization of jobs within a medical practice. An HR professional may be responsible for recruiting allied health jobs (e.g., those in radiology, lab, pharmacy, respiratory therapy, cardiac rehab, and other clinical areas), but not "nonmedical jobs" (e.g., finance, MIS, HR, and maintenance). This classification allows for better focus on certain types of positions.

A staffing plan sets in place the types and number of employees needed in a certain work group to achieve stated goals and objectives. This plan may flex based on office productivity, but has a core of staffing requirements. In a medical clinic, there may be the need for one RN, two medical assistants, a medical receptionist, and one file clerk. The flex staffing may be more or fewer medical assistants, based on the workload.

In addition, a position may be classified as either exempt or nonexempt, meaning that the position is salaried or hourly. In addition, a position can be full time (usually 36-40 hours a week), part time (usually less than 36 hours a week), as needed (ongoing, but less than 20 hours a week), temporary (usually less than 120 days), or student (learning).

Responsibilities

An employee may have formal and informal lines of responsibility. For example, a medical assistant may report directly to the director of nursing but work indirectly for the physician the director supports on a daily basis. These interactions and reporting relationships are important to note so that the employee is aware of the dynamics of the position. Many multi-site organizations are moving to a matrix level of reporting, in which a person reports to two different people – a site supervisor and a department supervisor. For example, a lab technician reports to the site supervisor and the regional laboratory manager. Again, the employee needs to know to whom he or she reports, and the job description should list the employee's supervisor by job title, not by supervisor's name. For example, a file clerk may report to the manager of medical records, and a triage nurse may report to the director of nursing.

Working Conditions

The job description should include working conditions in addition to duties and responsibilities. Working conditions help to set the stage for the environment that the employee can expect. A clerk may work in a cubicle all day in front of a computer and rarely need to stand. In contrast, a nurse may work with a computer in a nurse's station by the exam rooms and need to stand and walk for multiple periods of time. A file clerk usually has to be able to lift up to 25 pounds of boxes of files, or a nurse may be required to lift a patient from a bed to a gurney or from a wheelchair to a chair or the toilet. Working conditions provide the employee with a clearer expectation of what is required to perform the job appropriately.

Working conditions also help to explain the general safety hazards and environment in which the person will be working. General office working conditions with minimal hazards are very different than working outside on construction projects with heavy equipment.

Equipment Operated

Equipment operated helps to define some, but not necessarily all, of the equipment that a person may operate, including a fax machine, copy machine, computer, radiology and lab equipment, and cleaning equipment. Some equipment requires a special level of certification or education for proper operation.

■ Discrimination Issues

Americans with Disabilities Act (ADA) Issues

The Americans with Disabilities Act of 1990 is a federal civil rights law designed to prevent discrimination and allow people with disabilities to participate fully in all aspects of society. A fundamental principle is that people with disabilities should have an equal opportunity to work. The ADA defines a person with a disability as "an individual with a physical or mental impairment that substantially limits one or more major life activities," such as walking, hearing, seeing, and so forth. The disabled person must also be able to perform the job that he or she wants or was hired to do with or without reasonable accommodation. When a medical practice develops a position description, the position description needs to comply with ADA requirements.

Equal Employment Opportunity (EEO) Issues

The U.S. Equal Employment Opportunity Commission enforces the federal laws passed that do not allow a person to be discriminated against in terms of employment based on race, color, religion, sex, national origin, disability, or age. The laws that they enforce include[7]:

- Title VII of the Civil Rights Act of 1964 (Title VII);
- Age Discrimination in Employment Act of 1967 (ADEA);
- The Immigration Reform and Control Act of 1986 (IRCA);
- Equal Pay Act of 1963 (EPA);
- Titles I and V of the Americans with Disabilities Act of 1990 (ADA);
- Civil Rights Act of 1991; and
- Sections 501 and 505 of the Rehabilitation Act of 1973.

Some companies have placed additional qualifications to these federal guidelines by adding "no employment discrimination based on sexual orientation." It is unlawful to discriminate against a person because of the above areas in terms of employment including hiring, firing, promotion, layoff, compensation, benefits, job assignments, and training. A medical practice executive needs to be keenly aware of EEO issues and their impact on the practice.

TASK 3 **Develop Employee Placement Programs and Facilitate Workforce Planning**

■ Staffing

STAFFING A MEDICAL OFFICE requires a strong understanding of staff skills and abilities tied in with organizational goals. Staffing numbers and mix need to be tied into the organizational goals. The types of staff needed relates to the skill mix and knowledge that the practice requires. Hiring a registered nurse for a physician practice was a popular approach in the past. Currently, a medical practice will assess the skills needed for a practice and may decide that a medical assistant, rather than a nurse, can perform the skills needed for the practice. The goal may be to have the person room a patient, take vitals, learn the chief complaint, and handle minimal patient education. This staffing assessment helps the practice to determine the best mix of skills and abilities for which to recruit.

New Staff

The timing to bring on new staff is always a challenge. Sometimes staff members complain that they are overworked and need additional staff. That overworked perception may be specific to a particular day, due to understaffed departments as a result of vacations, or from additional tasks that have been assumed due to a special, time-specific project. It is critical for the medical practice executive to assess the needs of a department and determine under what circumstances and timing the staff may need more help.

Some organizations have a structure and culture that does not allow certain staffing changes to occur. A medical practice with an exclusive registered nursing staff is not as open to considering hiring medical assistants or LPNs as would be a medical practice that already has a mix of medical assistants and RNs. A culture that only has physicians may not be open to hiring midlevel providers.

Alternative Staffing

Midlevel Providers

A midlevel provider can include a nurse practitioner, physician assistant, or nurse midwife, among others. If hired, a midlevel provider should function in a medical practice under the direction and supervision of a practicing, licensed physician. The supervising physician must have the appropriate training, experience, and competence to supervise the midlevel provider. The physician practice should determine if a midlevel provider would fit within the group and determine the types of duties and functions that he or she would perform. Many arrangements have failed due to lack of preparation for a midlevel provider and a clear definition of the roles and duties of that position in advance. Many practices have found that the consumer patient rates midlevel providers very high due to their focus on patient education and the longer time that the midlevel provider gives to the patient.

Midlevel providers can be accepted in one physician specialty or region of the United States, but not accepted in another specialty or region. The use of a nurse midwife in an OB/GYN practice is common, but a midlevel provider may be less common in a region of the United States where malpractice rates are high. Strategically, the medical practice executive should determine whether the use of a midlevel provider would work from many perspectives, including economic, operational, and strategic.

Part-Time Employees

Part-time employees can help the medical practice address changing practice needs. A part-time employee may be able to flex hours based on the patient load or have the time to cover employees who are on vacation, sick, or being trained. A part-time employee may want to grow into a full-time position, but may want the flexibility of fewer hours now and more hours later.

Outsourcing

Staffing costs or restrictions may require a medical practice to outsource certain functions. Common outsourced functions may be information technology services, housekeeping, maintenance, coding, and billing. These functions, as outsourced services, have their own set of deliverables and expectations. Outsourcing may be able to achieve greater cost savings than if those services were performed in-house.

◼ Recruiting from Inside the Organization

A medical practice that posts all positions internally prior to posting them externally has a "promotion-from-within" philosophy. This approach conveys to the workforce that it values hiring from within prior to considering external candidates. Usually a position is posted internally for several days and those candidates interviewed prior to external candidates are considered. Some medical practices will post the position internally, concurrently post the position for the external marketplace, and hire the best-qualified candidate.

Sometimes an internal referral is the best way to find a new staff person. An employee will usually refer someone who is thought to be a good worker because referring an unproductive worker will reflect poorly on that employee.

■ Recruiting External Candidates

Advertising Strategy

There are limited dollars to advertise job openings. The medical practice executive determines how that money will be allocated. Newspaper ads in local and regional papers, television commercials, Internet banners, magazine ads in professional journals, and direct mail are all examples of advertising strategies that medical practices have used to recruit new staff.

Temporary Agencies

Temporary agencies can provide staff needed for a time-specific project or activity. They can also be resources for permanent employees. Hiring temporary agency staff allows a medical practice executive to determine whether a person possesses the necessary skills to perform the job on a continual basis and could fit within the organizational culture. Usually, if a company wants to hire a temporary agency worker, the agency charges a placement fee, which could be as much as 100 percent of the employee's first year's salary.

Internet Job-Posting Services

With the growth of the Internet, jobs can now be advertised on the medical practice's Website. An Internet search for a specific job or organization will bring up the job posting. This type of resource simplifies the job search for prospective candidates.

Search Firms

A search firm is a professional service provided to a medical practice to attract, hire, and develop staff who will hold jobs that are key to achieving the medical practice's goals and objectives. The service is paid by the medical practice, not the hired person. Possible job candidates are presented to the medical group by the search firm based on employer-specified requirements. The use of a search firm is meant to save the medical practice executive's time and money because identifying, qualifying, and reviewing potential candidates can be an expensive effort requiring tremendous effort.

When a search firm is hired on a contingency basis, that firm will earn a fee only if a job candidate is hired and retained by the medical practice. A "headhunter" is a common term used for a contingent firm because the majority of the firm's effort is based on getting the potential candidate in front of the medical practice.

In contrast, hiring a retained search firm means that the medical practice has a signed contract with the firm to hire a candidate, and these two groups work exclusively with each other to find that person. Also, the search firm is paid in advance, in whole or in part, prior to the candidate being hired.

Regardless of the type of search firm contacted, the medical group and firm must correctly fit the potential job candidate with the skills needed for the job and achieve a satisfactory hiring outcome.

Community Placement Services

A community placement service helps to link prospective job candidates to interested employers. These services may focus on working with students, new graduates, or displaced workers. The placement service is able to help the prospective job candidate develop a skill base, enhance the candidate's resume, help him or her gain a better understanding of various job opportunities within the community, and develop networks and support systems of people who can provide letters of recommendation, references, and possible job options.

■ Selection

Human resources must be fair and consistent in its hiring practices. A person who starts working in the medical practice without following any of the procedures or policies may engender a complaint being filed by other co-workers. Common mistakes are failing to post a position internally, failing to complete an employment application, or a person starting to work without having completed a drug screen or health physical. Even if the need to fill a position is urgent, it should never be done at the expense of following the process accepted by the medical practice. It is critical that the medical practice executive follow all legal practices and comply with all rules and regulations toward fair hiring practices.

There is a basic process for employee selection and customized applications, depending on the position:

- *Employment application form.* The application is the same regardless of the position. An application should be completed prior to conducting any interviews. The application will ask for information such as demographics, education, work history, references, and criminal record. The employee will sign the application, indicating that the information is correct and authorizing a release to the medical practice to verify the information.

- *EEO factors (e.g., advertising, recruiting, recordkeeping).* Careful records should be kept for any position being recruited. If a person later files a complaint against the medical practice due to violation of EEO factors, the practice would want to demonstrate that its process was fair and consistent, and complied with the law.

- *Interviewing (screening, behavior-based).* Screening interviews may be held on the telephone to determine the candidate's level of interest and skills for the position. Behavior-based interviews present the candidate with scenarios and ask how he or she would respond to those situations.

- *Panel interviews.* A panel interview may be a peer interview by people with whom the candidate potentially would work.

This approach builds consensus from the co-workers and allows them input into the process.

- *Open-ended questions.* Open-ended questions require more than just a "yes" or "no" answer. They encourage the candidate to discuss issues and share information about his or her background, experience, skills, and abilities, so that the employer can determine if the candidate will be a good fit for the position.

- *Testing (written, performance).* Some positions require a written or performance test to demonstrate competency in a job requirement. A medical secretary who is required to type 40 words a minute would take a typing test, or a file clerk would take a test showing the ability to file alphabetically and numerically.

- *Reference checks.* A job candidate consenting to reference checks allows the employer to talk to other people about the candidate and ask questions without fear of being sued or risking legal action. Some previous employers will give out only limited information, including the employee's position title, starting and ending dates of employment, and rate of pay. Others will answer questions about a past employee's quality and quantity of work, time and attendance, customer service background, and whether the employer would rehire the employee.

- *Criminal investigation and background checks.* Questions on the job application ask the potential employee if he or she has ever been convicted of a misdemeanor or felony. An official background check is usually conducted after an employment offer and prior to the employee's first day of work to verify that the employee doesn't have any undisclosed criminal history.

- *Offer of employment.* An offer of employment is usually made to the candidate with some time specified before a response is needed. If the position is accepted, a written confirmation is sent to the candidate confirming title, rate of pay, contingencies of employment, and start date.

■ *Health information and physical exams.* An employment offer may be contingent on the person providing health information and passing a physical exam. There may be a pre-employment drug physical to verify that the person is drug-free. Failure to pass any of these tests may result in the employment offer being withdrawn.

■ Benchmarks

The number of staff needed can be tied into benchmarking data of like organizations. A new physician will not require two new staff members, and a pediatrician practicing at the 90th percentile of production may need more than two staff to support the practice. The number of staff should be based on productivity measures, hours of operation, skills required, available technology, and other resources within the group. For example, a practice that has an EHR and automated telephone response system in place may not need the same number of staff as a practice of the same size that has paper medical records and no telephone automation.

Full-time equivalent (FTE) ratios provide a benchmark for the medical practice to follow. They may be guidelines or measures of productivity, production, and/or efficiency. For example, 4.5 FTEs per physician may be a good ratio for a physician achieving production at the 99th percentile, but a bad ratio for a physician at the 10th percentile. FTE ratios can help the medical practice guide staffing decisions and outcomes.

The Medical Group Management Association provides resources that benchmark physician-to-staff ratios based on numerous factors, such as physician specialty, medical ownership, and practice size. A busy family practice physician seeing 40 patients a day will require more staff than a busy urologist seeing 15 patients a day due to the volume of patients seen in a primary-care vs. specialty-care practice. In addition, the staff ratio needs to be broken down with respect to the types of people needed to assure that the appropriate mix of staff skills is available to support the physician.

Planning workforce needs is both an art and a science. Staff ratios may meet benchmarked data, but they still may be ineffective if the staff members are not well trained and other resources of automation, coordination, and teamwork are not in place.

■ Changes in the Organization and Market

Jobs evolve over time, and new types of jobs may emerge. A medical practice needs to change with the times and be open to employment changes based on the needs of the practice. Twenty years ago, no one in a medical practice would have considered having either a chief information officer (CIO) in a medical practice, or a telephone triage nurse. However, with the growth of information technology and automated applications, a CIO may be needed to handle the complexities and management of these applications. With the growth of managed care, requirements for preauthorizations for certain medical procedures and hospital admissions, and a more sophisticated and educated patient population, a telephone triage nurse can help address many of these new issues.

Expectations also change over time. A medical secretary hired to transcribe medical notes and answer the telephone for a physician may need to change job functions when "talk technology" eliminates the need for transcription and a call center is developed to answer the telephone. An employee who doesn't adapt well to change will become a liability instead of an asset when change is required within the practice.

Shortages in the labor pool create tremendous strain on the medical practice and may limit the practice's ability to meet current or growing patient needs. With a shortage of radiology technologists, a medical practice may not be able to expand hours of operation in the evenings or weekends. A strategy will help the medical group decide how aggressive it wants to be in recruiting hard-to-find staff.

■ Plans

Strategic and Business Plans

A strategic plan followed by a detailed business plan will help a medical practice to address its changing needs over time. A strategic plan usually is created for a 3- to 5-year period and articulates the practice's vision for the future. For example, the medical practice may have an aging medical group and need to recruit younger physicians. The vision of physician recruitment should be integrated into a business plan for the recruitment process. Planning for the future helps the medical group to become proactive and not reactive to a changing environment.

If a medical practice is open eight hours a day and five days a week, the space is used only 24 percent of the time. If a medical practice wants to expand its productivity, it can either see more patients every hour or expand its hours of operation. Developing a second medical office location for the practice can be an expensive endeavor unless the practice decides to pilot a new location through a time-share arrangement in which a physician shares space with another physician who already has an established practice.

Human resources may lead a strategic effort toward disseminated authority or may require decisions to be made by a board of directors or senior physician/administrative leader. Because the human resources department is a cost center, careful consideration is made on what the cost and benefits are for a particular decision.

Budget Plans

Eighty percent of a medical practice's budget may be focused on staffing. This creates huge challenges for the medical administrator to provide qualified, well-trained staff at a competitive price. A medical practice executive should consider how overtime, shift differential pay, and employee status (part time vs. full time) impact the bottom line in short- and long-term budgets.

■ Staffing and Scheduling

Staffing is both an art and a science. Developing an effective schedule based on staffing mix, hours needed, and skills performed will work if there are enough staff members to draw from. A mix of full-time, part-time, and as-needed staff who can work days, evenings, and weekends provide scheduling flexibility for the practice manager.

Schedules can vary based on physician or patient needs. Medical practices may vary employee shifts and hours based on employee preferences. For example, an employee may be attracted to three 12-hour shifts because it allows that employee to be off four days during the week, even though the employee has to work long hours for three days. In contrast, another employee may want only 8-hour shifts due to limitations in day care. Even though flexible schedules are logistically challenging, they can be strong employee satisfiers. Rotating employee shifts to work every third weekend may be preferable to required weekend shifts every week. These flexible schedule blocks can meet employee needs and meet the needs of the organization to provide staffing during nontraditional hours.

TASK 4 **Establish
Employee
Appraisal and
Evaluation
Systems**

■ **Employee Performance Review Methods**

Performance Standards

Numerous resources are meant to give the employee consistent feedback and expectations for performance. The employee handbook (see Task 7) will provide standard information, and a procedure and policy manual will give specific detail on the handling of a particular situation. The position description is a road map for an employee's expectations. It shows the overview, but isn't prescriptive. The employee objectives are the directions on how to reach a certain destination. Often an employee is given measurable objectives to meet, for example, file 30 charts per hour, order all supplies weekly, and enter all physician charges in the computer system on a daily basis.

The performance appraisal process should be job specific. The employee's actual job performance must be assessed during the appropriate feedback period, and comparisons made to key job responsibilities as written in the job description. Performance measures describe the actual level of performance for each of the dimensions included in the appraisal, with specific examples and written comments to validate the ratings. An example may be "Customer Service Orientation," with scaled ratings from "completely unsatisfactory" to "exceeds expectations." The customer service orientation would include teamwork, attitude, behavior, interpersonal skills, and problem-solving abilities. Each rating on the scale would define that level of service. Poor customer service orientation could mean that the employee is unresponsive to patient needs and does not respond well to supervisor recommendations for service improvement.

New hires may have a probationary period of 90 to 120 days to provide time to become trained and oriented to the new job. If the new employee doesn't meet the standards within the time frame, he or she can be terminated without following the typical progressive disciplinary policies.

If employee performance is contingent on educational updates and the employee has failed to become current, the supervisor must determine whether the gap stems from lack of employee motivation or organizational bureaucracy.

Annual Evaluations

A person's appraisal should be conducted at least annually based on objective criteria. Based on how well a person performs, these criteria should be tied to the person's wage increase.

Annual evaluations should be documented in writing, occur face-to-face, and occur on time. If an employee doesn't meet the minimum standards for performance in a specific area, a time-specific, written work plan should be developed with the employee. These plans may be called performance improvement plans (PIPs), action plans, or performance plans. Periodic feedback meetings should occur until such time that the standard is routinely met or until the end of the re-evaluation period. If the standard is not routinely met after appropriate training, orientation, and feedback, a progressive discipline policy should occur.

Evaluation Tools

Most large organizations have a standard evaluation tool. There also may be various tools based on the employee's job classification. Differences may exist for jobs that are patient care-related vs. clerical, exempt vs. nonexempt, and technical vs. professional. A smaller organization may not have a template or form to follow; rather, it may use a checklist of core competencies that are expected, such as lab proficiency, meeting documentation guidelines, and achieving core customer service skills. Evaluation tools are as varied as the organization, but all require basic components. Forms should be completed by the supervisor and signed off by the employee. The form should include specific time frames for the evaluation, the name of the person being evaluated, and the title being evaluated. Supporting documentation, such as an employee self-evaluation and manager comments, should be included as well.

Evaluation tools can have numerous formats. An open narrative tool allows a general essay-type format, but is open-ended and prone to subjectively. A scored evaluation, with points assigned to specific criteria, allows more objectivity. A self-evaluation tool, when used as part of an overall evaluation, allows the employee to participate in the process and contribute to a more complete evaluation. An employee's opinion of his or her own performance, however, may not be aligned with the expectations of the supervisor.

A 360-degree (or peer review) evaluation involves the supervisor, co-workers, and direct reports, as well as the employee, and creates a more comprehensive evaluation. This type of evaluation is a time-consuming process and usually does not involve all levels of employees. A select group of employees, such as management, is usually chosen for this type of evaluation.

■ Job Promotions

A job promotion could be a change in job duties and functions, or could result from additional responsibilities added to a current job. A promotion may or may not result in a change of job title or job pay. A promotion recognizes that an employee has performed well within an organization and is acknowledged by the organization with new, different, or additional responsibilities. Many times, a promotion comes after an employee has achieved a new skill set, for example, an employee who has earned a business degree or a medical assistant who has become a certified coder.

Regardless of the type of promotion, the process for a promotion should be fair and consistent. All new positions should be posted internally within the organization and list the skill sets required for the position. Even though there may be a preferred candidate, other employees should be allowed the opportunity to bid for the position. If a person doesn't meet the required skill set, he or she is not eligible for the position. It would be expected that positions with higher levels of education and responsibility would be tied to higher levels of compensation. Also, an orientation to the job as well as the organization is a wise way to help the new employee to succeed in the position.

Overall, a well-organized employee appraisal and evaluation system usually results in better employee satisfaction. Satisfaction is founded in respect, trust, fairness, consistency, and recognition. A well-built system will create a strong culture of performance and avoid the risk of an employee lawsuit. The goal of any system should be to create a culture of service excellence with a team of high-performing employees. The employee appraisal and evaluation system flows from the organization's vision and mission. Overall, the goals and objectives of the organization will align with the performance expected to achieve those outcomes and the rewards associated with those outcomes.

■ Informal Benefits Program and Rewarding Performance

Whereas certain aspects of a practice may be formalized, such as its benefit plan or written procedures and policies, employee recognition may be informal by allowing each department to provide employee recognition through its own program, such as employee meetings with paid lunches and provision of gift certificates for excellent performance or perfect attendance.

Awards

Organizationally sanctioned compensation includes traditional merit increases, annual bonuses, and approved administration of benefits. Special awards may involve employment tenure through service awards. An employee with five years of employment may receive a special certificate and gift, and a 10-year employee may receive a certificate and nicer gift. Everyone may participate in an awards banquet. Other special awards could be "Employee of the Month" or "Nurse of the Year," based on objective criteria.

Employee suggestion programs are common and allow the employee to evaluate job, department, and organizational functions and recommend suggestions for improvement. These suggestions, if implemented, may allow the employee to receive a wide range of rewards. Low-end rewards are gift certificates and money, whereas high-end rewards may pay the employee a percentage of the cost savings over a year.

Unsanctioned compensation may apply to a physician who decides to pay an employee a bonus when others do not receive one, or provide a dinner certificate for excellent service where no program exists. Although these generous efforts may benefit the employee being recognized, they may lower employee morale due to a lack of opportunity for others to receive comparable benefits.

Rewarding Desired Outcomes

Research has shown that money is not the key satisfaction factor mentioned by employees. Other key factors include a challenging and rewarding job that makes a contribution to the organization and recognition for a job well done. A written note given to an employee acknowledging excellent service and behavior is not only beneficial to the employee – the employee usually will share this commendation with co-workers, who then learn quickly what is expected and acknowledged.

In addition, a supportive manager, respect and trust, and positive communication are key requirements for a satisfied employee. Assuming that an employee's pay is competitive in the marketplace and aligned with the person's skills and experience, rewarding desired outcomes takes many forms. A merit-based performance valuation allows high performers to receive a higher monetary increase than average or low performers.

Some groups provide the same monetary increase for all employees regardless of performance. These increases serve more as "cost-of-living" increases than they do "pay-for-performance" recognition. Some medical groups provide an employee bonus at the end of the fiscal year based on how the employee performance contributed to the practice performance. This method can be highly effective in motivating employee groups to high performance. Some medical groups have employee programs that reward individual performance on a periodic basis. These programs, such as "employee of the month," "star performers," or "above and beyond the call of duty," may reward the employee with a recognition certificate or trophy, meal or gift certificates, and public recognition. These kinds of programs can be very positive if they are administered consistently with nonbiased, objective criteria and truly acknowledge excellent behavior and performance.

TASK 5 **Develop and Implement Employee Training Programs**

EVERY MEDICAL PRACTICE, if it wants to gain market share and become or remain successful, must provide its employees with continuing education. Whether it is pursued through internal means (staff meetings, training sessions, etc.) or through external means (association meetings, consultants, paid training sessions), continuing education builds a solid foundation of knowledge to better perform jobs. Every practice needs its employees to have continuing-education updates on safety (OSHA, universal precautions, fire prevention, and the like) and compliance (e.g., HIPAA, correct billing practices, and so forth) along with updates on technology and regulatory changes (e.g., Medicare, Medicaid, state laws). Continuing education may also be needed to keep an employee licensed or registered in a particular profession.

The medical practice needs to determine, in advance, what it will pay for training for the employee. Employee training can be very costly, but is usually worth the investment. The costs can usually be higher if the practice *doesn't* invest in its employees through lost productivity, citations, violation fees, fines, and other risk management issues.

For training to be effective, it must address a positive environment for learning, the quality of the materials provided, employee motivation and incentives to be trained, and adult learning models based on the group being trained. Training must be staffed by trained professionals as opposed to experts in content material and by people who can teach adults and provide different learning modes. Training is an investment in the medical practice and its results can be tied to the medical practice's performance.

■ Organizational Operations/Practices

Philosophy of Training and Development

Medical practices need to be aware of the ongoing changes facing the practice of medicine. To keep up with the changes in reimbursement, coding, managed care, compliance, and clinical practice, the employer must provide the employee with appropriate formats for learning. With the proliferation of technological advances, the medical practice executive should look at new options to improve results and outcomes. The medical practice and its employees are becoming more sophisticated consumers and are demanding better access to information. The employee demands more professional development opportunities, better access to those resources, and greater flexibility to learn.

The human capital for the medical practice is very important, and this recognition is critical in developing resources to meet the needs of the current workforce. The medical practice must be proactive in recruiting, managing, and retaining the best people to meet the organization's mission, goals, and objectives. To this end, it is critical for the medical practice to ensure that its employees have the necessary skills, resources, and abilities to perform their jobs. The diversity and variety of training opportunities will help the employee to see how the medical practice culture is conveyed through its training resources.

Training Value to Organization

The value of training to the organization can be measured through integration with appropriate evaluation tools. Evaluation tools are quick and objective ways to identify the strengths and weaknesses of the learning done. Evaluation is drawn from the employee evaluation, participant learning, achievement of the behavior change sought, and the overall impact on the organization. Accomplishment of these areas provides the demonstrated value of training and shows how it can impact the medical practice's revenue and profit, employee satisfaction, market share, and patient satisfaction.

Present Cost vs. Future Investment

Training is a budgeted line item, and its impact is measurable by future outcomes. For example, a medical assistant who performs charge entry must be familiar with CPT® and ICD-9 codes and needs to have knowledge of appropriate documentation for billing. Effective training will help the employee to question mistakes and capture possible lost charges or incorrectly coded charge tickets. A medical biller may be able to handle billing error follow-up better if he or she is trained on the correct coding edits and how to communicate with front-end staff on how to avoid these kinds of errors. This training will lead to faster payment and fewer errors to track. The cost to handle errors will be less, so the staff can focus more energy on doing things correctly than on fixing mistakes. Failure to provide training up front will result in poorer performance and outcomes in the future.

The medical practice executive should plan for employee training and determine who is eligible, how training needs are determined, and how those services are obtained. Reimbursement may be prepaid or paid after successful completion of the program. Tuition coverage may be a separate benefit to provide employee training or may be used to allow an employee to pursue higher education in a field that would benefit the medical group, such as business, nursing, or allied health.

Scheduling for Training

Freeing up staff to be trained is a logistics challenge. Time must be budgeted to allow staff to be appropriately oriented and trained.

Creative scheduling and flexible staffing are needed to accommodate and allow all staff to be trained.

Replacement Schedules

Depending on the size of the medical group, staff may be specifically hired to cover schedules of other staff when they are being trained. Replacement schedules allow staff members to be focused on the training at hand with the knowledge and comfort that their shifts are being appropriately covered.

Release Time

A medical group needs to determine under what circumstances an employee will be allowed company time or paid release time to attend an educational program.

Overtime Considerations

Although the goal is to use part-time and as-needed staff to cover staff being trained, there are times when staff will need to work overtime to accommodate the training needs of the organization. Overtime may need to be used for large-scale training projects, such as computer conversions, implementation of an EHR, or new equipment.

Paid Attendance, Meeting Time, and Continuing Medical Education Policy

Paid attendance may be specifically defined and there may be a cap on dollars or days available for training. For example, a physician may be given one week of continuing medical education (CME) days paid by the medical group not to exceed $3,000 per calendar year. This guideline helps every employee to manage expenses and time away from the practice appropriately.

■ Types of Training

Training content determination is a multidisciplinary group process. Usually groups identify more topics and issues than what can possibly be covered. Teams can help prioritize topics and level of detail needed for training, and this, in turn, largely determines the type of training to be pursued.

Orientation

All employees receive a general orientation to the organization. Usually, there is a general overview of the medical group, its practices and policies, and then a departmental orientation. These orientations can take hours or weeks to complete, depending on the complexity and level of detail needed for the employee.

Supervisory/Management

A management development program that creates a guide and/or template for the new manager to follow allows the manager to be aware of those areas that he or she needs to know within the organization prior to completing a full orientation.

Technical/Skills

Depending on the nature of the job, an employer may train the staff on technical and skill-based employment functions. Or they may expect a core level of technical and skill-based knowledge, but train the employee specifically on the organizational-based skill needed for the job.

Career Development

An employer may support an employee through career development opportunities. The employee may be afforded the opportunity to seek additional training and career advancement at the employer's expense. The long-term expectations of the employee must be clearly stated prior to the employee seeking these educational opportunities.

Certification

Certification allows the employee to demonstrate a core competency or knowledge in a specific field of study. Certification provides acknowledgment of skill, knowledge, education, and proficiency achieved in an area. Sometimes certification is required for initial employment or to continue being employed in the medical group.

Cross-Training

Cross-training a staff member allows the staff to be flexible in staffing schedules and allows staff to take time off without the worry of how the employee's tasks will be performed during the employee's absence. It also allows multiple people to be involved in a task and provide creative suggestions and ideas on how to improve a system or process. However, if cross-training is not done well, a person may assume a task and perform the task poorly through learned bad habits or behaviors. Cross-training must be continuously evaluated to ensure that employees provide quality in the work performed.

■ Adult Learning Styles

Employee training programs can be developed and implemented by the medical practice or can be outsourced to other agencies, schools, or organizations that focus on specific topics or issues. Training programs can take on many different forms to help the adult learner. An adult learner generally approaches learning differently from a young student. The adult usually is more self-guided in learning, brings more experience to the learning process, expects more from the learning experience, and will challenge any learning that doesn't make sense.

Learning by Doing

Many people learn best by doing. A medical assistant can learn all about how and why and under what circumstances to draw blood and about the tools needed to perform the function, but there is nothing like practicing on oneself and others to learn. Learning by doing can be invaluable as long as there is a written plan to demonstrate proficiency and competency in a learned function.

Didactic Teaching

Common classroom settings, which nearly every American has experienced at some time through formal education, provide a lesson plan, reading, class interaction, possible homework, and a test to measure whether the adult learner has mastered the skill or body of knowledge.

Mentoring and Coaching

Mentoring is a method of supporting a new employee to learn new tasks and duties from an exceptionally performing employee. Sometimes mentoring supports a current employee who is interested in learning new job tasks or functions. Mentoring must be carefully planned because some employees are exceptional employees but poor mentors or trainers. Some people know how to perform a job well but do not know how to show someone else how to do the same job. A mentor should be an active listener who is patient, willing to explain things repetitively, and able to break down job tasks into smaller segments and describe how they fit together. Many times, a mentor can become the company trainer or coach.

Coaching provides individual one-on-one attention to an employee needing greater supervision and encouragement. Coaching is a cyclical process that works with the adult learner and determines what kind of support the employee needs depending on the personal traits of the employee. The coaching support will depend on what part of the cycle the employee is in with respect to the task being mastered and learned. Usually, the new employee is a beginner and is usually enthusiastic to learn a new skill, but may be apprehensive about making mistakes. The learner needs clear instructions, constant feedback, emotional support, and praise when a task is learned well.

The next level of coaching is providing a lot of technical and emotional support for the employee so he or she is not discouraged from performing a task due to mistakes made. Also, poor technique should not become learned; bad habits can be difficult to break. Once the employee has learned the new skill, the coach provides guidance to reinforce the skill learned until the employee has mastered the skill and has become an expert. At that point, the employee needs little direction or support. The employee embraces the new task, takes ownership of the task, and begins to take on new tasks and responsibilities, and the coach can begin to work with the employee on new skills. Coaching helps to build employee confidence and affirms that the employee is performing aspects of the job correctly. Coaching also provides positive reinforcement of a job well done.

Self-Directed Learning

With the proliferation of computer technology, numerous self-directed learning modules can support an employee to learn new tasks and functions independently. These programs comprise reading, example problems, case studies, and questions to answer prior to taking a test. A self-directed program can be very effective for a well-motivated, organized adult. If the adult struggles with self-motivation, organizing and/or prioritizing workload, and/or using computers or reading booklets, a self-directed program may not work well.

Group Interaction

Providing a forum for group interaction can be a powerful and effective way for an employee to learn. Group interaction can promote personal growth, teach professional skills, and provide a cost-effective method to learn tasks and skills. The learning can be customized based on the particular group brought together. The group interaction can be based on small work groups, large forums, workshops, or even computer online Internet classes with dialogue forums.

■ Training Formats

Computer Media

Computer-based training allows the employee to use specific software on a self-directed basis to learn a new skill. The employee must have a basic level of comfort with computers to perform these tasks. Videos were very popular for training purposes during the last two decades; now, interactive videos in a VHS or DVD format are available on Internet and intranet sites. The low cost for this technology, when compared to staff travel and per diem costs, has made it a convenient venue for training.

Interactive Training

Interactive training allows the employee to participate in the process and learn by doing. A phlebotomy training class that allows the employee to practice drawing blood is more effective than just reading a book. Interactive training may involve a "skills lab" where employees can work in a simulated setting (e.g., patient exam room, telephone for customer service skills).

Role Playing

Role-playing exercises allow the employee to test practical knowledge learned in a real-life situation, but in a manner that is safe and protected. For example, a manager may learn how to have a "critical conversation" with an employee about poor work performance. The role play would allow the manager to talk with a trainer who pretends to be the disgruntled employee. Trying out different situations allows the manager to see whether the learned skills can be applied practically in a situation. The trainer provides feedback and constructive input on areas that can be improved in this situation.

Lecturer

A lecture or speaker presentation is another common educational format that is popular with large groups of people. The speaker may use overheads or handouts to cover the material and allow questions either during the presentation or at the end.

Group Discussion

A group discussion allows people to ask questions and hear different perspectives about an issue or topic. The group discussion may be focused on a series of questions that are asked of the group after the presentation of materials. Getting the group involved helps to affirm the topic and reinforce the knowledge.

Books

Books, workbooks, resource manuals, training manuals, and other printed material have been the most traditional resources for training. However, with the development of the Internet and Web-based applications, more books are being placed online.

Education Technology Online

Educational resources are now available online. A participant can log on to any computer with Internet access and take a class. The technology will monitor modules completed, tests taken, and completion of the training program. These applications make training much more accessible, convenient, and flexible. Many applications provide the participant with videos to watch and even provide opportunities to submit information and written materials for the reviewer to evaluate.

Outsourced Training

The use of outsourcing vs. an in-house training staff depends on the needs of the organization. Usually, the larger the organization, the more likely the medical group will pursue an in-house training staff. Smaller medical groups do not have the ability to hire someone full time to handle in-house needs.

An outsourced training program can be efficient, cost-effective, and provide a strong service level for the customer because the client provides these services routinely to a large group of employees. Outsourcing allows the medical practice to focus its energy on other aspects of the operations. Every physician practice has a limited number of human resources staff, whose services are focused on serving the employees and improving service excellence. With outsourced training, a physician group can use the best practices, systems, and educational venues with a smaller investment than creating, maintaining, and improving an in-house training program.

For certain areas, however, as a medical group expands and grows, there is value in having an in-house staff. A medical practice executive may bring certain training functions in-house (e.g., computer training, compliance, and safety training), but continue to outsource other training functions (e.g., cardio-pulmonary resuscitation, CPT® training). Regardless of the decision made, a physician practice must evaluate and discern how in-house and outsourced training will be used to educate employees.

Training the Trainer

Training the trainer allows a medical group to have one person or a group of people trained on a specific application or area of training and then bring that information back to the organization for on-site training and implementation. It can be project-specific (e.g., EHR implementation), department-specific (e.g., nursing orientation), or organization-specific (e.g., information technology, technology, computer, and clinical training). The trainer needs to be comfortable with using adult learning principles and focus on a program that develops objectives, selects the appropriate training method, develops training aids, and uses facilitation and problem-solving skills. In addition, a mechanism should be in place to evaluate the training sessions.

■ Desired Outcomes

Whatever the venue or approach toward training, medical groups should develop a process that will achieve its desired outcomes. The employee must be made aware of the topic, acquire the knowledge, change behavior, and achieve desired results. The medical group should improve the quality of learning for its employees and reduce course work and training time in an environment of limited resources. Even though more resources are available now than ever before, with the proliferation of computer training, the numerous options are confusing and it is difficult to stay focused on those core competencies that need to be achieved.

Training will continue to be a challenge for all medical practice executives until there is a focus on improving performance to achieve practice goals as opposed to solely increasing skill and knowledge. It is common for medical groups to assume that training is the outcome or solution without fully understanding the cause of the problems being addressed.

**Establish
Employee
Relations and
Conflict
Resolution
Programs**

ESTABLISHING EFFECTIVE EMPLOYEE RELATIONS and appropriate conflict resolution programs are necessary to work
toward common goals. The word "team" is overused in
health care – it conveys the expectation that everyone
will work together to accomplish a common purpose.
Often, employees and departments experience conflicts
that thwart the attainment of high performance. When
this happens, the supervisor needs to get involved and
talk with the employees one-on-one or in groups to identify the problems and determine a resolution. Sometimes
an objective third party may need to get involved if issues
are plagued with cultural or historical resistance or the
process of change isn't supported by the physicians. Also,
another party may need to get involved if the conflict is
between the employee and supervisor. Differences in
problem-solving styles, information processing, and communication can create conflicts that, if not resolved soon
after identification, may produce disastrous results.

■ Personnel Policy

The personnel policy should state which representative will resolve the issue. It may be the human resources representative, the medical practice executive, or an employee and labor relations consultant, or, if the practice is unionized, the union steward. This person will meet with the employee, supervisor, or both, as may be appropriate to the chain of command, to help in resolving their differences. This representative can provide advice on matters of policy interpretation, rights of management and employees, and information on the formal grievance process.

The personnel policy may have a statement on protection against retaliation of the employee for exercising his or her rights under the arbitration process. There may be time limits on the process to facilitate speedy resolution of the problem while providing appropriate time to collect, prepare, and present information. For example, if the employee fails to follow the time limits, the issue may be deemed to be resolved to the employee's satisfaction. If the medical practice fails to follow specific time limits, the employee may take the complaint to a higher level of resolution. Personnel policies should reflect current federal, state, and local employment laws.

Policy Interpretation for Grievance Procedures

For all disciplinary action, policy interpretation is a human resources responsibility. The disciplinary action or progressive discipline process is meant to give appropriate feedback to the employee in a formal way. This constructive feedback for desired results is meant to provide the employee with measurable accomplishments, instill individual accountability and responsibility, and facilitate the desired behavior. The supervisor can serve as a mentor, coach, and facilitator of the process and help the employee understand the desired results (see Task 5).

If the communication requires multiple areas of behavior change, the supervisor may choose to give the employee a Performance Improvement Plan (PIP). This tool focuses on below-average or substandard performance and provides an action plan for needed change. The plan is time-specific and allows the employee to receive periodic feedback. For example, an employee may receive a PIP for inappropriate interactions with patients. The PIP would provide the employee with customer service training and weekly feedback sessions between the supervisor and employee on improvement in the desired results. Failure to achieve desired results can lead to additional disciplinary action up to and including termination. The PIP's intent is to help the employee be successful and shepherd the process along the way.

■ Mediation

Mediation allows the employer and employee to troubleshoot issues and come to positive relations. It allows problems to be dealt with promptly and provides an opportunity to address a problem before it escalates into an unworkable issue. Usually, mediation will move away from blame or judgment and allow a win-win situation, as opposed to a win-lose situation. The two parties, not the mediator, control the situation and the outcome. Mediation can be used prior to a formal grievance process, such as arbitration. Using mediation, however, does not waive one's right to use a formal grievance process if the parties cannot reach a satisfactory outcome through mediation.

In mediation, a professional mediator contacts the two parties involved and seeks to achieve agreement. Usually, each party meets individually with a mediator first to identify and discuss the concerns. The mediator will keep all information from these sessions confidential. Then the mediator will bring the two parties together to discuss the concerns, and will work toward a win-win outcome. Sometimes a second session may be required, depending on the complexity of the issue. If the two parties reach an agreement, the mediator will work with them to create a written agreement listing the specific components of the agreement, which both parties will sign. Usually, these agreements do not change existing medical practice policies or union contracts.

■ Arbitration

Nonbinding arbitration is a way of avoiding disputes because it provides a written guide on the practice used in employee grievances. The purpose of the arbitration policy is to establish a procedure for the fair, orderly, and speedy resolution of disputes that sometimes arise between management and employees. The policy will state to whom it applies (e.g., all members, unclassified employees) and how the policy is used. An employee may use the procedure to review an alleged violation of the medical practice's policy or rules pertaining to employment.

In a nonbinding arbitration process, two parties give a dispute to a neutral person to determine an advisory or nonbinding decision, meaning that neither party is required to accept the opinion. In the process, the two groups have input into the selection of the person arbitrating. Nonbinding arbitration is used when the parties want a quick dispute resolution, prefer a third-party decision maker, and want more control over the decision-making process if not resolved. In binding arbitration, both parties present a dispute to an impartial arbitrator to determine a binding decision. The parties have the ability to decide who serves as the arbitrator. Binding arbitration is appropriate when the parties want a neutral third party to decide the outcome of the dispute and avoid a formal trial. The parties do not retain control over how their dispute is resolved and cannot appeal the arbitrator's decision.

■ Employee Grievance Procedures[8]

Initially, there should be an attempt at an informal resolution of complaints. Regular communication between the practice managers and employees reduces the need for a more formal review and is in the mutual best interest of the medical practice and employees. Written resources materials, handouts, and guides should always be available to help management communicate information with employees. An employee who has a work-related problem should bring it to the medical practice executive's attention with the intent of resolving the problem. In a timely manner, management should discuss the concern with the employee with an effort to resolve the issue. If informal attempts at resolution are not satisfactory, employees may use a formal grievance process.

Listening to employees is key to assuring excellent performance. Active listening will help to identify whether any issues or concerns are preventing the employee from performing the expected job duties. Early identification of problems can avoid serious problems later. If, through active listening, a supervisor recognizes that a problem exists that requires a higher level of problem solving or counseling, the supervisor needs to recognize his or her limitations and refer the employee to either the Human Resources Department, or, if offered, an Employee Assistance Program (EAP), to help the employee sort through personal issues that are inhibiting acceptable performance levels.

■ Progressive Discipline

What does discipline mean to an organization? Corrective action strives to provide feedback to an employee to correct a behavior. Progressive discipline sets parameters on which behaviors are unacceptable and how the negative behaviors requiring change will be communicated with the employee. Large medical groups usually have a progressive discipline process that clearly establishes expectations and consequences of those behaviors if not met. The discipline process may be different for the staff and physicians. The purpose of having a constructive discipline process is to establish guidelines that will assure an environment that is efficient, productive, and orderly to provide standards and rules governing performance and a procedure for consistent, nondiscriminatory application of the rules with the intent of providing quality patient care. The policy does not apply to employees who are in their new hire period or per diem or temporary employees. The personnel policy applies to part-time and full-time regular status employees.

Progressive discipline must be fair, consistent, well understood, and timely. Lack of a consistent process to administer discipline may ultimately lead to a disgruntled employee filing a lawsuit. A progressive discipline program provides the employee with feedback that clearly outlines unacceptable behavior and the consequences if this behavior is not changed. Usually progressive discipline involves a verbal warning followed by a written warning. If behavior doesn't change, a suspension or final written warning is the next level of discipline. Ultimately, if behavior doesn't improve, the employee may be terminated. Some behaviors may warrant a progressive level, and other behaviors may warrant more, or may skip a step and move into a higher level of discipline. For example, chronic tardiness would go through progressive discipline, whereas stealing money would result in immediate termination or suspension, pending an administrative investigation. Employees must understand that there is a process for discipline and consequences to bad behavior.

If a union is present in a practice, the union's progressive discipline process may require a union representative to be present with the union employee and manager when progressive discipline is administered.

Recorded Conference

For rule infractions considered less serious, a recorded conference may be the first step in the corrective action process. It consists of a verbal conference with, at a minimum, the employee and supervisor and will be documented in writing and placed in the employee's personnel file. Examples of behavior for which a recorded conference may be initiated as the first step of the correction action process include:

- Work area absence without permission (e.g., leaving work without clocking out);
- Extended lunch time or breaks without permission (e.g., taking a 30-minute break instead of a 15-minute break);
- Loitering during scheduled work time or during off-duty hours (e.g., staying in work area after shift and creating disturbances with employees);

- Smoking or eating in unauthorized areas (e.g., eating in surgical area that is a sterile environment);

- Conducting personal business on work premises (e.g., selling products during work time);

- Violation of parking rules (e.g., parking in a "no parking" or "patients only" zone for the duration of a work shift);

- Improper attire or appearance (e.g., wearing jeans or denim when not part of the dress code);

- Inefficiency or incompetence in work duties performed (e.g., failing to perform job duty during work shift);

- Unauthorized telephone use (e.g., making long-distance or extensive personal calls without permission); or

- Attendance problems (e.g., showing up late for work without prior notice or permission).

Written Corrective Action

The written corrective action is a document summarizing the performance problem or incident detrimental to the customer, inability to follow established policy, or the failure to respond to supervision. A written corrective action serves as notice that continued infractions will not be tolerated and/or that performance must improve to meet expectations. Examples of behavior for which a written corrective action may be initiated as the first step of the corrective active process include:

- Inappropriate treatment or behavior toward a customer;

- Conduct prejudicial to the best interest of the medical group;

- Careless, indifferent, or negligent job performance, including unsafe or unsanitary practices;

- Careless, neglect, unauthorized, or improper use of company property or equipment;

- Collecting money or accepting gratuities for personal use;

- Failure of good behavior or neglect of duty; or

- Repeated or chronic infractions with no evident improvement in performance or conduct.

Suspension or Final Written Corrective Action

An unpaid suspension or final written corrective action in lieu of suspension may occur when performance continues to be detrimental to customer satisfaction or where a serious performance problem exists. Suspensions should be scheduled at a time as close to the infraction as possible but also so that patient care and consistency of service do not suffer. Depending on the seriousness of the incident or behavior, the employee may receive a suspension or final written corrective action as the first step of the corrective action process.

Examples of behavior warranting suspension include possession, use, or sale of alcohol, narcotics, or controlled substances on the medical group premises, or reporting to work under the influence of alcohol or narcotics, usually evidenced by one or more of the following behaviors:

- Inability to perform assigned work;
- Presentation of undesirable attributes (e.g., hygiene, attitude, uncooperativeness);
- Insubordination or refusal to perform a reasonable assignment after having been instructed by a supervisor to do so;
- Sleeping on the job;
- Disorderly conduct;
- Failure to conform to professional standards; or
- Any other critical failure of good behavior or serious neglect of duty.

Termination

Termination may occur as the final step in the corrective action process. Termination of an employee is never an easy task, but it is a necessary one if the employee does not consistently follow the medical groups' policies and procedures. Termination may occur for serious offenses or for continued performance problems impacting the customer. Examples of behavior where immediate termination may be initiated as the first step of corrective action include:

- Threat of or actual physical or verbal abuse of patients, visitors, employees;

- Inappropriate treatment of any patient for any reason;

- Falsification of any official medical group records (e.g., medical records);

- Illegal or dishonest act;

- Damage or theft of property;

- Absence from work without justifiable reason or, in some practices, without reporting off for two (or more, depending on the practice's variables) consecutive working days;

- Unauthorized possession, use, copying, or revealing of confidential information regarding patients, employees, or medical group activity;

- Unwelcome sexual advances, requests for sexual favors, or other verbal or physical conduct of a sexual nature with an employee, visitor, or patient;

- Harassment in any form, including that based on race, gender, religion, or national origin, which includes offensive jokes, ridicule, or racial, religious, sexual, or ethnic slurs;

- Improper use of leave of absence;

- Conviction of a felony relevant to the employee's position;

- Solicitation and/or distribution of literature (e.g., pornography, political campaigns, etc.); or

- Any other gross neglect of good behavior or gross neglect of duty.

■ Employee Assistance Program

In today's changing workplace environment, the medical practice executive is expected to provide more services with fewer dollars. Employees are expected to do more tasks and handle stressful situations professionally. This stress may cause worry, confusion, doubt, and even sickness. Dealing with prolonged stress may cause fatigue, depression, anger, and anxiety, which may lead to defensiveness, inappropriate behavior, and co-worker conflict. Although some worry and anxiety is normal, sometimes these emotions can become problematic and impact employee productivity, lower employee morale, and foster poor outcomes. An Employee Assistance Program helps the employee stay on track and provides coping mechanisms to perform better in a state of uncertainty.

An EAP is a medical practice resource that uses a comprehensive program of counseling services for employees and/or their dependents to help improve employee and workplace effectiveness. It provides confidential, third-party counseling and work/life services to employees in an off-site setting, and its effectiveness is through its efforts toward prevention, identification, and resolution of employee personal problems that impact employee productivity. EAP services may be provided by the employer's own EAP program or provided through an external agency. The EAP program is not a mandated employee benefit, yet it can be very beneficial in reducing employee risk, cutting costs for recruitment of new employees, and improving employee productivity. Employees may use EAP for counseling or further referrals for financial counseling (e.g., bankruptcy, money management, gambling), family issues (e.g., death, divorce, separation), domestic violence (e.g., spousal or child abuse), alcohol and substance abuse, mental health issues (e.g., depression, suicidal ideation, phobias), and family law (e.g., adoption, custody, restraining orders). The medical practice executive may use EAP to help employees better address issues that impact poor performance, provide an on-site counselor in case of a traumatic event (e.g., employee death), or provide on-site training to handle employee issues more effectively.

An EAP may be needed by an employee as a further condition of employment. If the employer believes that the employee cannot continue working in the medical practice without EAP services, then it becomes a mandatory referral. However, most EAP services are sought by the employee voluntarily. EAP services usually are available to all part-time and full-time employees, regardless of employment position.

EAP and Counseling

Counseling for Emotional Issues

On a basic level, it is important for an employee to have good emotional health. EAP provides support to employees and helps them to address emotional issues. The physician, medical practice executive, or HR director is not a trained therapist. When it is determined that the dialogue with an employee is moving from sharing feelings to needing help in managing emotional issues, an EAP referral should be made. The staff is not equipped to handle professional counseling issues and should not attempt to provide such counseling.

Family/Marital Counseling

Numerous family issues may prevent an employee from completing work accurately or on time for the medical practice. Persistent feelings of dissatisfaction may impact the workplace and create disruptions. Counseling can help to address problems with a child's behavior, school adjustment or performance; difficulties with anger, hostility, or violence; family stress due to illness; stepfamilies dealing with stepchildren; and ex-spouses.

Financial Counseling

Employees may have financial problems that may distract them from their work and create decreased productivity. A troubled employee may distract other employees and ask for help from co-workers who are not qualified or have the skills necessary to help the employee. Typical financial areas may include issues with debt, money management, credit, and consumer and retirement planning.

Legal Counseling

Legal counseling can help the employee to address legal issues, clarify goals, find appropriate counsel, and address appropriate legal costs.

Career Counseling

Employees can get stuck in a rut or a job with no future. Career counseling can help the employee to gain help in career planning by addressing:

- How to conduct a self-assessment;
- How to address career advancement options;
- How to identify skill development opportunities;
- How to write a resume;
- How to interview;
- How to identify available continuing-education workshops; and
- How to cope with transitions in a job function or duty.

EAP and Potential Workplace Violence

According to the U.S. Bureau of Labor Statistics' Census of Fatal Occupational Injuries (CFOI), there were 639 workplace homicides and 8,787 fatal work injuries in the United States in 2001.[9] The medical practice physicians and staff need to have the required skills to identify, prevent, minimize, and eliminate violent and aggressive behaviors. EAP can help a medical practice to develop an effective program that brings management commitment and employee involvement together to create an environment that has a zero-tolerance policy on workplace violence.

EAP and Stress Management

Stress is neither good nor bad. It is how we manage stress that makes a difference on our bodies and mind. Negatively managing stress can create feelings of anger, depression, distrust, paranoia, and rejection; and result in health problems, such as high blood pressure, insomnia, rashes, headaches, and upset stomach. Any change can create stress in an employee's life, from a new job to managing a heavy workload to a death in the family to a new relationship. EAP can help the employee to better manage stress, as opposed to eliminating stress.

EAP and Tolerance for No-Solution Situations

Sometimes an employee may be faced with a no-solution situation. EAP can help the employee accept what can be changed, what cannot be changed, and what the employee can do to cope with these situations. As long as the employee is able to perform on the job based on the goals and expectations of the practice, the employee's success is based on his or her ability to handle stress constructively.

EAP and Age Discrimination

Change is inevitable in any medical practice. However, some workers stay in the same job for years. As new management or physicians come into a practice, they may institute change that is perceived as trying to eliminate the employee. Employee comments such as, "We've always done it this way, so why do we need to change" and "I'm too old to handle this kind of stress anymore" are indicators that the employee may perceive discrimination due to age. EAP can help the employee address change in a positive way and help the employee see that age is not a factor when experiencing change.

EAP and Objectivity

An EAP program is meant to provide an objective stance on an issue facing an employee. EAP provides perspective and help where the employee may perceive that help is not available in the practice. For example, when a work-related issue arises, an employee may have difficulty handling criticism and indirect challenges of not performing. EAP can help the employee to address these issues from an objective perspective.

During times of stress, an employee may turn employee issues away from self-review and focus energy on others. A common reaction is the sense that a policy interpretation and its follow-up are unfairly administered and have not been applied fairly. EAP can provide an objective view and interpretation of those policies.

EAP and Substance Abuse/Impaired Physicians

Substance abuse may result in immediate termination or a mandatory referral to EAP to seek necessary outpatient or/and inpatient treatment. Failure to seek mandatory treatment would result in immediate termination. A medical practice may have an "Impaired Physician Committee" to handle problems and concerns revolving around a physician's behavior or clinical competence during times of stress. The committee may address physician issues pertaining to substance abuse, health status, violence, sexual harassment, and mental status. All these issues may affect the physician's ability to care for the patient on a professional level.

■ Unions

The Wagner Act of 1935, otherwise known as the National Labor Relations Act (NLRA), was passed to protect employees' rights to unionize. The National Labor Relations Board (NLRB) was created to implement and enforce the NLRA. Numerous labor laws are currently in place; however, the Wagner Act marked the federal government's initial support for unionization and collective bargaining. The NLRB conducts elections to determine whether employees want union representation and also examines unfair labor practices by employers and unions. The act guarantees employees the right to self-organize, choose representation, and bargain collectively.

The NLRB must also make sure that employers do not discriminate against union members. Labor laws allow employees the right to unionize and to participate in strikes, picketing, and lockouts to have their demands met. Employee areas for consideration may include employees' amount of pay, pay methods, benefits, work hours, type of work performed, and qualifications required. It may also involve the workers' physical proximity and integration of tasks, the employer's supervisory or medical practice structure, and specific employee preferences. For example, union issues could involve the physical proximity of a group's work area to facilitate interaction among group members. If the work area was split across two floors of the same building, a union could see a negative impact on the group. The lack of proximity of the work spaces can create disintegration of work tasks and have a negative impact on the group's ability to perform its job, and therefore can be perceived as a burden on the workforce.

Union-Free Workforce

For a medical practice to maintain a union-free workplace, it must be experienced in knowing how to combat union organization efforts. The medical practice executive's human resources function, along with legal counsel, can help the medical group address local union activity, organizing tactics and targets, early warning signs of union involvement, lawful employer countermeasures, effective personnel policies and practices, and the employer's legal rights in dealing with a union. The medical practice must provide its front-line supervisors and/or managers with the training necessary for lawful union avoidance. Managers must know what they can and cannot say about unions and unionization, and how they must communicate effectively with the employees they oversee. The practice executive should know how to effectively exercise the medical practice's legal rights due to assertive union campaigns, including how to lawfully communicate critical facts about collective bargaining, union dues, member obligations, strikes, and shutdowns to all employees; and how to deal with union campaign handouts, postings, speeches, and videos that are lawful. Usually, the consideration of a union is due to a lack of effective communication and problem solving with employees to address proper and effective employment practices.

Union Grievance Procedures

If a union has been established in a medical practice, the union contract will specify the grievance procedures. The process may be very similar to that for nonunion employees, although it is best to read both policies for confirmation.

Competitive Wages

Unions will dictate a competitive wage package and a schedule for wage increases. Commonly, the program does not provide merit increases, but rather a fixed increase for each union employee.

Communication Plan

When the union and the medical practice sign a contract, there is a communication plan to ensure that the union employees understand the agreement on the practice's procedures and policies.

■ Conclusion

Establishing effective employee relations and instituting conflict resolution programs are important functions in a medical practice. They provide for better communication between employee and employer and allow for opportunities to address grievances and employee issues. A medical practice executive should have a working knowledge of HR laws and regulations, grievance procedures, progressive discipline, and programs to help employees to be productive.

Maintain Compliance with Employment Laws

HUMAN RESOURCE POLICIES provide a framework for both the medical practice and the employee. These policies allow the medical practice to direct its employee relations and articulate what is expected, and the policies should prevent any misunderstandings about employer policies.

Employees often do not know their rights and responsibilities and may receive bad advice from co-workers or friends. An employee handbook that spells out the medical practice's procedures and policies can help provide each employee with guidance on what is considered an "acceptable" practice and well within the law.

Smaller medical practices may not have the range of written policies and procedures that a larger practice will. Regardless of practice size, the medical practice executive is responsible for ensuring that all appropriate laws and regulations are observed and followed. Failure to do so may result in inconsistent and noncompliant practices and cause for a potential lawsuit.

Employment law is complex and requires a keen awareness to ensure compliance. A medical practice executive may need support from an attorney or HR consultant to ensure compliance with all appropriate laws. A periodic external review of current practices to ensure compliance with the law will demonstrate a commitment toward compliance. Written policies should be reviewed by legal counsel to ensure that they reflect applicable federal, state, and local requirements.

A well-run medical practice will be up to date on the various labor relations issues that may impact a practice. Whether this is done through an experienced human resources professional, outside legal counsel, or the medical practice executive's own efforts, he or she should be knowledgeable on a range of issues, from requirements on minimum wage, workers' compensation, unemployment compensation, to unions, collective bargaining, and fair employment practices.

■ Employee Handbook

Every medical practice should have an employee handbook, which is given to each employee with the expectation that he or she signs a statement indicating its receipt and agreement to abide to its policies. The following lists the topics that typically would be included in a handbook:

- *Medical Practice Welcome.* Welcome statement from a key leader; a disclaimer that the information in the handbook is not all-inclusive;

- *Introduction.* Mission statement, career opportunities, and code of conduct;

- *Employment.* Equal employment opportunity; employment eligibility; eligibility for employment; nepotism; criminal convictions; violence and use of weapons; alcohol, drugs and illegal substance abuse; sexual and other harassment; employee evaluations; access to one's personnel file;

- *Policies and Procedures.* Attendance; parking; work schedule requirements; bulletin boards; time cards; lunch and other breaks; dress code; compensation and overtime; taxes, FICA, and Medicare; performance and evaluation reviews; reporting personal information changes; gifts, entertainment and meals; visitors; personal property; personal safety; smoking; drug testing; noncompete and nondisclosure agreement;

- *Company Property.* Confidential information security; office supplies; postage and company accounts; phone systems; voice mail and personal calls; conservation and recycling;

- *Computer-Related Policies.* Computers and related equipment; use of the Internet and intranet; use of e-mail and electronic communications;

- *Policies for Leave of Absence.* Eligibility, personal and sick leave; unpaid leave; absence under the Family and Medical Leave Act of 1993 (FMLA); jury and military duty;

- *Benefits.* Health and dental insurance; pension; life insurance; and

- *Discipline Policies.* Progressive discipline; violation of company policy; termination of employment.

General Regulations

Wages and Benefits

From a legal perspective the medical practice follows the federal Fair Labor Standards Act, which requires a minimum wage of $5.15 per hour. This act also requires equal pay for equal work regardless of gender. Some states have enacted higher minimum wage requirements, but most medical practices pay employees more than the minimum wage.

A medical practice may not restrict benefits for employees of a like group. Benefits must be administered fairly and consistently. For example, if health insurance is available for full-time nonexempt staff, a medical practice may not indicate that one medical receptionist may have health insurance and another one cannot because that employee has insurance with a spouse. The benefit must be offered to all eligible employees. It is up to the employee to determine whether he or she wants, or even is eligible for, that benefit.

Performance

Performance or lack of performance and how that evaluation is communicated with the employee could result in an unsatisfied employee. If the employee can demonstrate that the performance review is discriminatory or has violated a certain law, the medical practice must be confident that its practices and process comply with the law.

Many lawsuits surround employees contesting a disciplinary action process that results in termination. It is critical that the medical practice have a written process that is consistent with the law and is administered fairly and consistently.

Safety and Health

Every medical practice must keep its employees safe from harm. The physician credo to "do no harm" to the patient must be extended to the employee in the workplace. The medical practice executive should work diligently toward employee and patient safety. The practice environment must be safe and comply with OSHA laws as well as with local zoning or building codes.

Fraud and Abuse

The U.S. Office of the Inspector General (OIG) carries out a broad range of duties nationally through audits, investigations, and inspections to protect the U.S. Department of Health and Human Services (HHS) programs and the beneficiaries of those programs. It has developed guidelines for individual and small medical practices toward the development and implementation of a voluntary compliance program that promotes adherence to any and all federal health care program requirements. Every medical practice has a duty and responsibility to ensure that its physicians and employees are knowledgeable and committed to following the rules and regulations of the federal government and that they know what those rules are. The guidelines include the following:

- Designating a compliance officer;

- Implementing compliance through written and well-communicated standards;
- Having practice-specific education and training;
- Communicating appropriately with employees, physicians, and others;
- Performing internal monitoring and auditing;
- Responding to compliance issues with appropriate correction action; and
- Enforcing sanctions for noncompliance.

Nondiscrimination

Medical practices may have a nondiscrimination statement that would prohibit discrimination in all of its activities on the basis of certain classes such as race, color, national origin, sex, religion, age, disability, sexual orientation, and marital or family status. Persons with disabilities who require other means for medical practice communication information, such as interpretation services, should contact the medical practice executive. Also, the medical practice executive should offer the person the ability to file a complaint of discrimination by providing an address and/or telephone number for the person to contact, if warranted. The medical practice usually would provide a statement in its internal publications that states "ABC Medical Practice is an equal opportunity provider and employer."

Payroll Records

Every medical group needs to keep records on its payroll practices. Based on the common saying, "If it's not documented, it wasn't done," medical practices need to have employees document the hours worked in the practice. Payroll procedures and policies should be established to ensure that a fair, consistent, and legal process is followed in paying employees the correct amount for the exact hours worked. There are particular laws that govern payroll practices, including that nonsalaried employees are to be compensated for overtime, and that time cards are properly completed and signed off by employees. In many organizations, inaccurately completed time cards can result in termination.

Employment at Will

Many U.S. states have an "employment at will" policy, which means that an employer may hire or fire an employee at will without any resource or reason. However, due to the numerous employment laws and regulations, an employer may have to prove that terminating an employee was not due to discrimination. As a result, the employer may need to indicate specifically why the employee was terminated.

State and Local Laws on Sexual Orientation

Sexual orientation laws have been developed by some states and localities, but not federally. A medical practice should be fully aware of its state laws and the respective requirements placed on the employer. In New York, for example, the Sexual Orientation Non-Discrimination Act of 2003 (SONDA) prohibits discrimination on the basis of actual or perceived sexual orientation in employment, housing, public accommodations, education, credit, and the exercise of civil rights. This latter protected category was newly added to various state laws, including New York's Human Rights Law, Civil Rights Law, and Education Law. Although a medical practice may choose to follow a certain law even if it isn't required in its particular location, it must follow those laws and their administration in those states where it does apply. This involves the medical practice executive knowing not just that the state law exists, but also how it is interpreted and implemented in that state. Usually, when a law is passed, numerous legal firms and HR consultants are available to provide advice on how to follow the new law.

Licensure/Certification

Certain medical professions require licensure or certification. The medical practice executive should ensure that the affected employees are appropriately licensed or certified and that their licenses are updated accordingly. For example, a physician's medical license is state-specific and requires renewal on a periodic basis. The medical practice executive needs to keep the physician's updated medical license on file because that is a requirement for employment. Failure to do so could result in a medical provider administering care without a license, and the concomitant sanctions against the practice for allowing the provider to do so.

Recordkeeping

Keeping accurate and timely employee records and files is necessary to maintain a well-run practice. From updated addresses and emergency contacts to completed tax forms and signed disciplinary action paperwork, the medical practice executive should provide diligent maintenance of employee records. Practical issues follow if the records are not kept up to date. In an emergency situation in which the medical practice building is without electrical power and the practice will be closed, employees need to be informed of the closure. If telephone numbers are not updated, a problem exists for contacting employees in a timely manner. Personnel records must also be up to date in case of a medical problem with an employee, such as fainting while on the job; without current records, it may take life-saving time to determine the possible reason for the fainting, such as an insulin attack.

■ Specific Legislation

Americans with Disabilities Act of 1990 (ADA)

The ADA prohibits discrimination and guarantees equal opportunity for persons with disabilities in employment. A medical practice must make reasonable accommodation for a disabled employee to perform his or her job. In addition, ADA specifies services for non-employees, including having handicapped-accessible restrooms and providing access to interpretation services for deaf patients or patients requiring a language interpreter.

The Family and Medical Leave Act of 1993 (FLMA)

FMLA requires covered employers to provide up to 12 weeks of unpaid, job-protected leave to "eligible" employees for certain family and medical reasons. Medical practice employees are eligible if they have worked for the medical practice for more than one year, for 1,250 hours over the previous 12 months, and if there are at least 50 employees within the medical group within 75 miles of the practice's main office (some employees may work off-site or at satellite clinics, but these must be within a 75-mile radius). In addition, FMLA allows employees to take leave on an intermittent basis or to work a reduced schedule under certain circumstances. This far-reaching legislation has tremendous employment impact for larger medical groups with more than 50 employees but does not impact smaller medical groups. By being legally required to hold a person's job for up to 12 weeks, the larger medical practice is challenged to find adequate and appropriate coverage during this time frame.

Occupational Safety and Health Administration (OSHA)

The Occupational Safety and Health Act of 1970 protects employees from harm on the job and has established a nationwide, federal program to protect the workforce from job-related death, injury, and illness. OSHA was developed within the Department of Labor to administer the act. OSHA has significant impact on a medical practice, especially in the areas of responsibility that include policies on blood-borne pathogens, emergency response, hearing safety, lockout/tagout, respiratory safety, lead safety, fire safety, office ergonomics, personal protective equipment, material safety data sheets, and right to know for hazard communication (HazCom) materials. A medical practice must be fully aware and compliant with OSHA regulations at the workplace. Complying with OSHA will help to provide the workplace and employees with a safe environment in which to work. A medical practice must have knowledgeable people well versed on OSHA, its requirements, and practical implementation of those requirements.

Civil Rights Act/Title VII

The Civil Rights Act of 1964 was passed to provide guidance on discriminatory practices, including discrimination due to race, color, religion, sex, or national origin. Title VII of the act covers specific information about such discrimination and other unlawful employment practices.

Immigration Reform and Control Act of 1986

The Immigration Reform and Control Act controls unauthorized U.S. immigration by instituting employer sanctions and penalties if aliens are hired who are not authorized to work in the United States. Every new hire in a medical practice needs to complete an I-9 form documenting through two approved source documents that he or she is not an illegal alien. A medical practice executive cannot cut corners by failing to have new employees complete this form.

National Labor Relations Act of 1935 (NLRA)

The National Labor Relations Act of 1935 (NLRA) guarantees workers the right to join unions without fear of management retaliation. The National Labor Relations Board (NLRB) enforces this right and bans employers from committing unfair labor practices that would deter organizing or prevent workers from negotiating a union contract. Employees have the right to self-organization, to be part of labor organizations, and to collective bargaining and its activities. Unions are discussed in more detail as part of Task 6 of this volume.

Equal Pay Act

The Equal Pay Act of 1963 is part of the Fair Labor Standards Act of 1938, enforced by the Equal Employment Opportunity Commission (EEOC). It prohibits sex-based wage discrimination between men and women in the same medical practice who perform duties under similar working conditions. If a court finds that the practice is in violation of this act, the judge can fine the group up to $10,000 and/or send the responsible party (e.g., the owner or the medical practice executive) to jail for up to six months. Gender should not be taken into consideration when paying an employee for work done in the medical practice.

Age Discrimination in Employment Act

The Age Discrimination in Employment Act of 1967 prohibits employment discrimination against persons 40 years of age or older. This act is meant to promote employment of older people based on ability rather than age, to prevent arbitrary age discrimination in employment, and to help medical practices find ways to address employment problems stemming from age issues. When hiring an employee, age should not be taken into consideration for older workers unless it can be demonstrated that age is a factor in preventing the employee from adequately performing the job.

Vocational Rehabilitation Act

In 1920, the U.S. Congress passed the Smith-Fess Act promoting states to give rehabilitation services to disabled veterans. Succeeding legislation has expanded the services and those who can receive them. The Vocational Rehabilitation program now operates under the authority of the Rehabilitation Act of 1973. Medical practice executives can work with agencies to determine how they can help support this program including ways to provide potential candidates with jobs.

Vietnam-Era Veterans Readjustment Assistance Act

The Vietnam-Era Veterans Readjustment Assistance Act of 1974 requires that employers with federal contracts or subcontracts of $25,000 or more provide equal opportunity for Vietnam-era veterans, special disabled veterans, and certain veterans who served on active duty. Although this law may not apply to medical practices, the medical group must be aware of the circumstances under which it may apply.

Pregnancy Discrimination Act

The U.S. Pregnancy Discrimination Act of 1978 indicates that discrimination on the basis of pregnancy, childbirth, or related medical conditions is unlawful under Title VII of the Civil Rights Act. A pregnant woman should be evaluated regarding her ability or inability to work and should not be terminated, be refused employment, or, conversely, be promoted because of a pregnancy.

Affirmative Action

Affirmative Action is the set of public policies designed to help eliminate discrimination based on race, color, religion, sex, or national origin. The medical practice executive can request that all potential employees complete a form indicating their backgrounds, which are independently summarized to demonstrate that the practice is considering all potential candidates regardless of race, color, religion, sex, or national origin. Sometimes a practice will list that it is an "affirmative action employer" to demonstrate its commitment to diversity.

■ Supervisory Training on Legal Requirements

A medical practice cannot assume that every new supervisor is knowledgeable about the various laws and requirements of the medical practice. An orientation to the law, its impact on employment, and implementation of those laws are required to demonstrate compliance with the law. Ignorance is no excuse – courts expect that all employers know the law.

Consequences for noncompliance with a law have serious repercussions for both the medical practice and the supervisor. Supervisor prejudice, employer bias, and ignorance can be costly for the medical practice and do not make good business sense. An educational program for new supervisors and an ongoing educational program for current supervisors will help ensure that everyone is current and up to date on correct employment practices.

Appropriate vs. Inappropriate Actions

Some common practices that can be inappropriate in terms of employment revolve around candidate interviews. Knowing the right (and wrong) kinds of questions to ask may seem simple, but in reality, it is quite complex. Questions about the candidate's age, marital status, and place of residence are appropriate for a health physical (which many physicians perform each day), but not for an employment interview. The medical practice executive can help supervisors know how to interview as well as learn what is considered an appropriate action vs. an inappropriate one.

Supervisory Responsibilities

A supervisor is responsible for following the law. Well-meaning intentions to "help out" an older worker by giving higher-paid work to a younger worker because the older worker might be tired, or not promoting a pregnant worker because she needs her rest while pregnant, will lead to employee grievances for discriminatory practices. If a supervisor is ever unsure of the correct practice, he or she should consult with the medical practice executive, who should be conversant with such laws.

Supervisory Review and Monitoring Functions

Management by expectation is a first start toward compliance, but management by inspection provides a practical way to demonstrate compliance with the law. Observing appropriate HR practices helps the medical practice executive know whether a practice is being followed and the areas for which additional education and training may be needed.

Measuring compliance with the law is another way to determine that all HR functions are being followed. Auditing personnel records for I-9 forms and completed employment applications, and reviewing whether all employees have received and signed receipt of the employee handbook are all important measures that the medical practice executive can conduct.

Documentation

Memory does not constitute documentation, nor does the statement, "I'm too busy. I don't have time to document." Documentation is the cornerstone of HR management and the medical practice executive's responsibility, and is a critical element for any follow-up needed on resolving any issue.

Investigation

Sometimes, the medical practice executive needs to conduct an investigation to learn further information before a final decision is made. For example, an employee may have completed the employment application by answering "No" to the question about "Have you ever been convicted of a felony?" However, a background check may reveal that the employee has a record with a conviction. The practice executive needs to investigate the accuracy of the data collected and interview the employee for further information prior to making a decision on any new data. Employee discipline and termination is another supervising function that cannot be overlooked. For further discussion on these skills, see Task 6. It is usually the policy of a medical practice to terminate an employee who has falsified information on an employment application.

Maintaining compliance with employment laws is accomplished through continuous review and monitoring of HR policies, procedures, and practices. By keeping current on practices that impact the medical group, the medical practice executive can align organizational needs with HR law. Attention to detail and commitment to compliance become part of the management culture and enable the medical group to function appropriately within the confines of the law.

Conclusion

CREATING AN EFFICIENT and effective human resources function is one of the most important activities in a medical practice. The medical practice has to care for its staff and attract and retain the best employees. The human resources function of managing employees and addressing their needs and wants is a constant challenge. A function that exclusively focuses on the employees without an organizational commitment to increase patient satisfaction through a cultural change, however, will ultimately fall short on improving service.

Human Resource Management must focus its commitment to a service culture that brings physicians and employees together to improve patient, physician, and employee satisfaction. A commitment focused on service to people (patients, employees, and physicians alike) fosters a transformation to service excellence. The medical practice that focuses its effort on excellent service will differentiate itself from the competition. The human resources function can help facilitate the accountability of that service from physicians, administrators, and staff. The shared commitment and cooperation of these groups is critical for a culture of service to evolve meaningfully and to make a difference.

A well-run medical practice with a strong vision, mission, goals, and objectives will use its human resource function to develop, implement, and maintain excellent programs in salary and wage administration, benefits administration, procedures and policies, recruitment, appraisal and evaluation, employee relations, training and development, and reward and recognition. The key to that success will be grounded in excellent service and quality patient care.

Exercises

THESE QUESTIONS have been retired from the ACMPE Essay Exam question bank. Because there are so many ways to handle various situations, there are no "right" answers, and thus, no answer key. Use these questions to help you practice responses in different scenarios.

1. You are the administrator of a medical group. The nursing director approaches you for advice on how best to respond to a complaint from a nurse about a verbally abusive patient. This nurse refuses to care for this patient because he uses language she finds vulgar and offensive.

   Describe how you would handle this situation.

2. You are the administrator of a group that has historically
    used registered nurses as its sole clinical support staff. You
    realize this might not be an ideal staffing model.

    Explain how you would evaluate your staffing mix and how
    you would implement any subsequent changes.

3. You are the administrator of a primary care practice that derives 40 percent of its revenues from capitated contracts. The group recently lost several of its physicians to active duty when their National Guard unit was activated. The group is unsure how to manage the capacity in the interim.

   Describe how you would handle this situation.

4. You are the administrator of a medical practice. A physi-
    cian-owner has demanded an increase in an employee's
    salary because he believes the employee is irreplaceable.
    The employee has indicated that she will leave unless she
    gets a raise. The supervisor's performance reviews of the
    employee do not justify the increase, however.

    Describe how you would resolve this situation.

5. You are the new administrator of a medical practice. The group does not have a formal wage administration plan. The physicians have set salaries for their own staff and have created disparate wages among similar positions. A female employee files a formal grievance that a male employee in a similar position with less seniority is being paid more than she is.

   Describe how you would handle this situation.

6. You are the administrator of an oncology group of four
    male and two female physicians. The office has two pods of
    exam rooms shared by male and female physicians. Each
    physician has one nurse to assist daily with the patients.
    One of the nurses left a note on your desk stating that she
    intends to file a sexual harassment complaint against one
    of the oncologists who works in the same pod. The nurse
    states that the physician constantly tells "sexist" and inap-
    propriate jokes to staff and patients.

    What course of action would you take in this situation?

7. You are the administrator of a multispecialty group with a primary care division. The general internist recently employed two physician assistants (PAs) as part of his delivery team. These new providers are allowed to refer patients to any of the specialists in the group. One of your cardiologists was not in favor of adding midlevel providers to the practice. In particular, he believes the PAs should not be allowed to refer patients without oversight from one of the internists. He has also made disparaging remarks to several of the staff about "inappropriate referrals" by the PAs.

Describe how you would you handle this situation.

8. You are the administrator of a 10-physician single-specialty practice. Three receptionists share the tasks of greeting patients, answering the telephone, scheduling appointments, and maintaining patient medical records. One of your group's board members has had conflicts with one of the receptionists. This physician has expressed to you on several occasions that he is unhappy with the receptionist's performance. He thinks that she is rude on the telephone, does not provide his patients with the level of customer service that he feels is appropriate, and has misplaced patient files. The physician has come to you demanding that the receptionist be fired.

    Describe how you would handle this situation.

9. You are the administrator of a four-physician single-specialty practice. All the nursing staff and the support staff report directly to you. You and the group's physicians report to the medical director. One of the junior physicians in the group wants a newly hired registered nurse (RN) to report directly to him and to support all of his actions. You have denied this request, given the group's established reporting structure. You have recently learned from one of the other RNs that the junior physician has sent the newly hired RN home early on light days, has authorized her to attend an in-state educational conference without seeking your approval, and has given her negative information about your management style.

Describe how you would handle this situation.

10. You are the administrator of a small single-specialty group practice and are responsible for all human resource issues for nonphysicians. You are currently recruiting for a front-desk receptionist whose responsibilities include greeting patients and collecting copayments. One particular job applicant appears to be an excellent candidate for this position. As part of your pre-employment process, you do telephone reference checks. During one, you learn that this applicant is very competent, but did not get along with two of her co-workers. The decision of whether to offer the position is up to you.

Describe how you would handle this situation.

11. You have recently been hired as the administrator of a 10-physician medical group. To understand the practice and find out more about the organization's operations, you hold interviews with each of your physicians. During the interview process, several of the physicians make comments concerning the skills of the billing office manager, who has been an employee of the group for more than 20 years. In the past week, you have received complaints from several of the staff that report to the billing office manager regarding inconsistent application of personnel policies and procedures. Morale in the billing department is quickly declining because some staff members have been offered flexible work schedules and some have not. In addition, it has recently come to your attention that collections are behind cash flow forecasts.

    What course of action would you take in this situation?

12. You are the administrator of a multispecialty group practice in which physicians have traditionally been paid a base salary plus a bonus based on charges. The same formula is used for all physicians. The primary care physicians are complaining that they are underpaid and treated unfairly under the current compensation plan and that their contribution to the organization as a whole is unappreciated. They claim that the formula to calculate the bonus should include a factor recognizing their direct contribution to the revenue generated by the specialist. You have been asked by the executive committee to outline a proposal for a compensation plan that incorporates relative value units (RVUs) that would be fair, consistent, and could be applied to all physicians.

Describe how you would handle this situation.

Notes

1. John C. Maxwell, *The 21 Irrefutable Laws of Leadership: Follow Them and People Will Follow You* (Nashville, Tenn.: Thomas Nelson Publishers, 1998), 17.

2. Stephen R. Covey, *7 Habits of Highly Effective People: Restoring the Character Ethic* (New York: Free Press, 2004), 101.

3. The MGMA book *Physician Compensation Plans* by Bruce A. Johnson, JD, MPA and Deborah Walker-Keegan, PhD, FACMPE, contains comprehensive details on this topic, including specific models for different types of health care organizations. More information about the book is available through the MGMA Store at www.mgma.com

4. U.S. Congressional Budget Office, *How Many People Lack Health Insurance and for How Long?* (Washington, D.C.: U.S. Congressional Budget Office, Health and Human Resources Division, May 2003).

5. CPT® is a registered trademark of the American Medical Association.

6. The MGMA *Job Description Manual for Medical Practices* by Courtney Price, PhD, and Alys Novak, MBA, contains job descriptions for most medical practice staff positions. More information about the book is available through the MGMA Store at www.mgma.com. MGMA members may locate a sample medical practice chief executive officer job description and competencies required, based on the *ACMPE Guide to the Body of Knowledge for Medical Practice Management*. This job description is available on the member section of the MGMA Website at www.mgma.com/members/infocenter/jobdescription.cfm.

7. U.S. Equal Opportunity Employment Commission, "Federal Laws Prohibiting Job Discrimination," www.eeoc.gov/facts/qanda.html.

8. Lawrence F. Wolper, *Physician Practice Management: Essential Operational and Financial Knowledge* (Sudbury, Mass.: Jones and Bartlett Publishers, 2005), 154, 160–161.

9. U.S. Bureau of Labor Statistics, "Census of Fatal Occupational Injuries (CFOI) – Current and Revised Data," www.bls.gov/iif/oshcfoi1.htm.

Glossary

401(k) Plan – Voluntary investment plan in which the employer defers employee compensation to a special fund for future use at retirement.

Arbitration – A process by which opposing parties present a dispute to an impartial arbitrator to determine a decision.

Americans with Disabilities Act of 1990 (ADA) – A federal civil rights law designed to prevent discrimination and allow people with disabilities to participate fully in all aspects of society.

Affirmative Action – A set of public policies designed to help eliminate discrimination based on race, color, religion, sex, or national origin.

Consolidated Omnibus Budget Reconciliation Act of 1985 (COBRA) – This federal employment insurance law that requires employers to provide a time-limited health insurance premium to any employee who leaves the organization.

Employee Assistance Program (EAP) – A benefit offered by employers that provides help to employees to address personal issues that may impact employee performance.

Employee Retirement Income Security Act of 1974 (ERISA) – A federal law that sets minimum standards for voluntary established pension and health plans to protect plan participants.

Federal Insurance Contributions Act (FICA) – A section of the Internal Revenue Code that requires a portion of a worker's paycheck to be deducted to support the Social Security and Medicare programs.

Family and Medical Leave Act of 1993 (FMLA) – A law requiring covered employers to provide up to 12 weeks of unpaid, job-protected leave to "eligible" employees for certain family and medical reasons.

Full-Time Equivalent (FTE) – A term used to describe the number of hours considered to be the minimum for an employee to work in a normal work week; this can be 37.5, 40, 50 hours per week, or some other standard.

Gainsharing – A reward system for increased productivity by which employee pay increases are based on organizational productivity or cost reductions.

Health Insurance Portability and Accountability Act of 1996 (HIPAA) – Health care legislation that mandates the safety, security, and protection of patient data, specifically addressing storage, dissemination, and access to protected health information.

Internal Revenue Service (IRS) – An agency of the federal government that taxes people and organizations for services.

IRS Code Section 457 – Nonqualified, deferred compensation plans established by state and local government and tax-exempt employers.

Job Task – A high-level function describing a key component of a position.

Mediation – A formal process in which a professional mediator works with two parties and seeks to achieve agreement.

National Labor Relations Act of 1935 (NLRA) – Legislation passed to protect employees' rights to unionize. The National Labor Relations Board (NLRB) was created to implement and enforce the NLRA.

Occupational Safety and Health Act of 1970 – Legislation that established the nationwide, federal Occupational Safety and Health Administration (OSHA) program to protect the workforce from job-related death, injury, and illness.

Pay Grades/Steps – Parts of a compensation system. A "grade" is assigned to a specific position based on the required skills, qualifications, and requirements needed for job performance. These grades are placed into progressive "steps."

PTO – Paid time off from work.

Profit sharing – A compensation system by which the employees of a medical practice receive a predetermined share of the organization's profits.

Severance pay – A predetermined amount of money, usually based on length of service within an organization, that an employee may receive if his/her position is terminated.

Strategic plan – A written document, usually created for a 3- to 5-year period, that communicates the medical practice's vision for the future.

Workers' Compensation – A state-mandated form of insurance covering workers injured in job-related accidents. In some states, the state is the insurer; in other states, insurance must be acquired from commercial insurance firms. Insurance rates are based on a number of factors, including salaries, firm history, and risk of occupation.

About the Author

Michael A. O'Connell, MHA, FACMPE, CHE, is Vice President of Operations and Physician Services of Huron Hospital in East Cleveland, Ohio, part of the Cleveland Clinic Health System. Previously, he served as senior director of Cleveland Health Network's (CHN) Management Services Organization (MSO), which supports the physician practice operations of Cleveland Clinic Health System and other CHN entities. He serves on the Ohio MGMA Board as the ACMPE Forum Representative and serves on the board of the Healthcare Executives Association of Northeast Ohio (HEANO), a chapter of the American College of Healthcare Executives.

Mr. O'Connell is co-author of a chapter on group practice human resources management in *Physician Practice Management: Essential Operational and Financial Knowledge*, published by Jones and Bartlett. He has a master of health administration degree from Saint Louis University, St. Louis, Mo., and a bachelor of science degree from the University of Illinois, Urbana.

Index